1Corinthians

I0143275

GARY R. SMALL

Print ISBN: 978-1-4866-2592-5
eBook ISBN: 978-1-4866-2593-2

Word Alive Press
119 De Baets Street, Winnipeg, MB R2J 3R9
www.wordalivepress.ca

WORD ALIVE
—P R E S S—

Cataloguing in Publication may be obtained through Library and Archives Canada.

Contents

Series Introduction

Keep this Book of the Law always on your lips; meditate on it day and night, so that you may be careful to do everything written in it. Then you will be prosperous and successful. (Joshua 1:8)

The word meditate and its derivatives occur eighteen times in the Bible. Of these, eight pertain to meditating on the Scriptures. Through these verses, we are encouraged to hold God's word in our hearts so that we might profit from His wisdom and be blessed by a closer relationship with Him (Psalm 119:1–3).

The secular world has also proposed the concept of taking a thoughtful approach to life and uses the word mindfulness to describe a thoughtful, meditative approach to life.

Mindfulness has been defined as "the awareness that arises through paying attention in the present moment, on purpose, nonjudgmentally."[1] Other terms have been applied to this intentional approach, such as *to internalize, to meditate on,* or *to process.* It is what we as Christians do when we carefully consider the Bible.

---

[1] Judson Brewer, *Unwinding Anxiety* (New York, NY: Avery, 2021), 71. Quoting Jon Kabat-Zinn.

The trouble is that we often don't have time to study in this manner. Instead we find ourselves snatching moments in our busy lives to read, internalize, and digest passages from our daily reading of the Bible. By squeezing these most important moments of the day into the least number of minutes, we don't make time for the mindfulness required to truly digest God's word.

Another mistake we often fall into is having too high expectations of ourselves. We lean into weighty commentaries or topical novels on life-changing subjects and once again find that we don't have the sufficient time or headspace to do justice to the meaty subjects therein.

We previously referred to this problem as having too much pace and not sufficient peace to make sense of God's word. It is the challenge that led to the production of this series of books, which are designed to help lift a word from His word and make it poignant.

How we choose to use the selected word for each chapter will be different for each reader. Each chapter is designed to provoke mindful thought on a biblical passage. We have also provided three applications at the end of each chapter to stimulate further reflection.

It is hoped that the chosen word from each passage will be recalled throughout the day when we find moments of stillness or thought, so we can pay attention, on purpose, nonjudgmentally.

These books can be used by individuals. They may also find use in group settings to provoke further discussion on a sermon series or in small group Bible study.

It is hoped that the books will be used as a spiritual tool to reinvigorate your Bible reading and provide impetus to make a life change as a Christian.

The concept is simple, one which by no means seeks to detract from the value of in-depth Bible study. There is still a place for this when time allows and further reading references are provided. We have taken care to tread a middle road theologically and avoid weighty arguments on some finer points of hermeneutics, although some of these can be found within the referenced material.

We sincerely hope that *A Word from His Word* will not only lift selected words from the pages of Scripture but also provide a lift to your Bible reading and spiritual life.

Much has been made by the secular world of the benefits of mindfulness. I suspect this discipline is not new, although it has perhaps been lost in our striving for scientific purpose. Yet there is, in this series, an opportunity to rediscover the usefulness of intentional meditation on God's word (Psalm 1:1–2).

Foreword

When we try a new food, there is a moment between when we taste it and our reaction. This is perhaps best captured on television food programs when chefs tempt a presenter with specialties from their restaurant. Once the presenter takes his or her first bite, we wait for the response. This is most often, and most naturally, a facial response—followed by an opinion. The moment of anticipation is fleeting, perhaps lasting one or two seconds.

When we taste anything that appeals to our senses, like the unveiling of a painting or the aroma of a new perfume, the anticipatory delay can be longer. We allow our senses to marinade in the new experience. Our first impressions are built upon by second and third impressions. Our first thoughts become flavoured by other aspects of the experience.

This is certainly true when reading a new book. After the first sentence or first paragraph, we might get a sense of whether we're going to find it easy going or a hard read. But as to whether we will enjoy it? That takes longer to judge.

Some biblical books are short, encouraging reads, useful for building foundations or encouraging persistence. Philippians, for example, comes to mind. On the other hand, 1 Corinthians is less well-read and is surrounded by an air of mystery. It's hardly ever discussed in its entirety. Instead sections are selected to illustrate a point or invoke a congregational response.

In view of its mysterious content, the delay in judgment as to how 1 Corinthians "tastes" requires a few chapters. It's certainly a rewarding read and the format of *A Word from His Word* encourages thoughtful reflection on both the passage and its commentary.

Inspirational and insightful explosions of taste come through from our reflections on Greek words, and the passages are punctuated with crisply served applications that come across as sympathetic wine pairings to complement each reading and prepare the reader for what comes next.

We find within 1 Corinthians foresight and wisdom from Paul, which he applies as Christian perspectives to matters that arise in a young church—and in young Christians. Since we are all young at heart, we readily perceive how Paul's words apply to our own lives and Christian walks.

I hope you will read 1 Corinthians in its entirety, using the bite-sized passages presented in this volume of *A Word for His Word*. Take the time to enjoy the moments between reading and responding. It is here where God speaks.

Don't rush the periods of anticipation between hearing His words in scripture, learning about them, and applying them. There is great value in the pauses.

Savour your moments with this edition of *A Word from His Word* and breathe in something of the hope Paul had for the young church in Corinth.

Introduction

Paul was working in Ephesus around AD 55 when he wrote 1 Corinthians. He had received a letter from the church in Corinth and been paid a visit by three members of the congregation. News of the church was mixed. It had survived and possibly grown in numbers since Paul's inaugural visit around AD 52.

Sadly, though, disagreements had arisen. Those conflicts seem to have been between individuals who held to the foundations laid by Paul versus others who had adapted Paul's message to be more in keeping with Corinthian culture.

Corinth was a busy metropolitan and commercial centre in southern Greece and considered second only to Athens. If Athens was the political hub, Corinth was the industrial centre. Corinth was Toronto to Canada's capital of Ottawa, or New York to Washington DC in the United States, or Glasgow to Edinburgh in Scotland.

Following Roman demolition in BC 146, Corinth had been rebuilt in BC 46 due to its excellent location. The city linked the Greek mainland with the Achaian peninsula and lay on an isthmus between the Corinthian and Saronic gulfs in the Mediterranean Sea. The isthmus was thin enough to allow the portage of small boats, or cargo could be unloaded onto mule trains for transportation. Both methods were used to avoid the sea journey around the Achaian horn.

Corinth was more than just a busy seafarer's town. It was famous for its commerce and the diverse goods passing from East to West and West to East. New goods were constantly arriving in the city, whether from the East and beyond into Asia Minor, or from the West and the outer reaches of the Roman Empire. It was a city of novelty and change.

It was also infamous for its immorality. Overlooking the city was the acropolis on which stood a temple to the goddess Aphrodite. Aphrodite was the Greek goddess of love, lust, beauty, and procreation. As a result of the activities of the multiple devotes alleged to live in the temple, the word Corinthian had become a synonym for people with liberal sexual morals. A trip to Corinth, whether or not on the pretence of business, was a risqué journey full of temptation.

Paul had arrived in Corinth from Athens (Acts 18). In Corinth, he met Aquila and Priscilla, who were also tentmakers. Paul initially both lived and worked with them.

At some point during Paul's tenure, the synagogue became upset with him. The leader, Sosthenes, seems to have been part of a Jewish delegation that tried to have Paul prosecuted by Galio, the Roman proconsul. This attempt failed and Sosthenes fell afoul of the Jews, who turned on him and beat him.

At a later date, or perhaps as a result of the treatment by his fellow Jews, Sosthenes appears to have become a Christian since he is also named as a coauthor of 1 Corinthians.

Paul recruited Aquila and Priscilla to the ministry. And when it was time for Paul to leave, they left with him and journeyed to Ephesus. During their stay in Ephesus, Priscilla and Aquilla helped to inspire and teach a Jewish man named Apollo who became a Christian. Apollo would later travel to Corinth and the Achaian peninsula to continue in Christian ministry.

Paul appears to have enjoyed his time in Corinth, since it was the place he ministered longest outside of Ephesus. During the eighteen months he stayed with the Corinthians, Paul became invested in their lives.

In this letter, Paul was magnanimous in his praise of Stephanas, Fortunatus, and Achaicus, those who had delivered the news concerning their church. In response, Paul saw the need to write, send Timothy, and begin to plan to return himself. His threefold response speaks to the dearness with which he held the church and to the preciousness of the gospel he wanted to see preserved.

Paul had brought change to Corinth when he delivered the good news about Christ.

He also challenged some worldly notions of wisdom and power. The cross, for instance, would be difficult for some to accept. At least on the surface, the crucifixion seemed to have spelled the end of a nascent religious movement.

In addition, he challenged people's beliefs about the afterlife, as well as their understanding of the importance of social standing. He also set limits on moral behaviour, since God's standards were not the same as those of Aphrodite.

The people of Corinth responded differently to these challenges. Some responded to Paul's message wholeheartedly and accepted Christ. Such individuals, like Stephanas, became Christian representatives in their community. They understood the breadth and depth of the message and adapted their lives accordingly. They embraced their new faith, grasping the dear cost that had been paid for their salvation.

Although others received Paul's news with enthusiasm, they were having second thoughts. Perhaps they were simply too stuck in their ways or too involved with Corinthian life.

Some may have converted to Christianity after Paul left and didn't fully understand the gospel that had been extended to them. The foundations of their faith hadn't been solidly laid. One can imagine that once church was over and normal life resumed, such people found themselves back to their old tricks and ways of life. Their commitment to this new faith could be easily broken because it had been formed under fragile circumstances.

When we reflect on these three groups—adherents, second guessers, and fragile flip-floppers—we see three different responses to the same message. We see successful change, good intentions without persistence, and no real attempt to change, and perhaps even hypocrisy.

God, in His merciful wisdom, leaves the decision of how to respond to us. He does promise to support us once we're on board, but the choice is ours (John 14:18, 26).

As an evangelist, Paul presented this choice in the form of the gospel. His message would have cut like the wake of a large boat through choppy seas. He sliced apart established religious thought, dismantling accepted cultural practices and societal norms. In the process, he disturbed the status quo and focussed the minds of those who would hear.

The wake of a boat follows in its stead, remaining behind or leeward of the craft. Depending on the size of the boat or the calmness of the water, the wake will persist for some time. This creates a still path in the water where the waves have been flattened and the passage is easier for those who follow.

As Christians, we all live in the wake of others. We live and practice our Christianity in the lee of those who taught us and by the power of the Holy Spirit.

Sometimes, though, just like the Corinthians, we feel the sea getting choppy again and we lose sight of the wake.

Paul wrote 1 Corinthians because he was keen to make sure the wake he left was strong, to make sure its course was clearly visible and remained true to the gospel.

It is useful for us as Christians to consider the wake we ourselves leave behind. Like Paul, we will want to be sure it's strong and able to resist the swell of the surrounding water. And like Paul, we will wish it to be consistent with the gospel, not full of half-truths or twisted currents.

Paul's message in 1 Corinthians was a call for the church to step back into the wake he himself followed: the wake left by Christ. In this, he highlighted the importance of unity.

We might more easily grasp the importance of this by considering the wakes left by multiple small boats all going in different directions versus that of a large ship ploughing its course. Only a unified church can effectively perpetuate the wake left by Christ, which remains the role of the church today.

Our challenge as we read this letter is to ask the question being asked of the Corinthians: are we not only following but also perpetuating the wake?

By spending intentional time with God by listening and reading *A Word from His Word*, my hope is that you will better discern the wake and will of God so we can travel homeward in unity. As we do so, may we leave a true and broad wake for others to find, appreciate, and use to travel home.

> The time of meditation does not let us down into the void and abyss of loneliness; it lets us be alone with the Word. And in so doing it gives us solid ground on which to stand and clear directions as to the steps we must take.[2]
>
> —Dietrich Bonhoeffer

> When you spend time with the Bible, you are fed, you are convicted, you are thrilled, you are inspired and you are fired up to proclaim it because it is God's Word. It is like charging a dead battery.[3]
>
> —Ajith Fernando

---

[2] Dietrich Bonhoeffer, *Life Together* (New York, NY: HarperOne, 1954), 81.

[3] Ajith Fernando, *The Call to Joy and Pain* (Nottingham, UK: Intervarsity Press, 2008), 143.

Enriched

1 CORINTHIANS 1:1–9

Paul, called to be an apostle of Christ Jesus by the will of God, and our brother Sosthenes,

² To the church of God in Corinth, to those sanctified in Christ Jesus and called to be his holy people, together with all those everywhere who call on the name of our Lord Jesus Christ—their Lord and ours:

³ Grace and peace to you from God our Father and the Lord Jesus Christ.

⁴ I always thank my God for you because of his grace given you in Christ Jesus. ⁵ For in him you have been enriched in every way—with all kinds of speech and with all knowledge—⁶ God thus confirming our testimony about Christ among you. ⁷ Therefore you do not lack any spiritual gift as you eagerly wait for our Lord Jesus Christ to be revealed. ⁸ He will also keep you firm to the end, so that you will be blameless on the day of our Lord Jesus Christ. ⁹ God is faithful, who has called you into fellowship with his Son, Jesus Christ our Lord.

At the beginning of any letter—whether a business letter, personal correspondence, or official address—there is a format to be followed. Paul followed his usual pattern. He introduces himself, gives thanks for the letter's recipients, and writes graciously.

All that is to be anticipated, but what catches our attention in this opening address is the reference to Jesus Christ in nearly every verse. It's as if Paul aims to centre the attention of the Corinthians on Christ. He wishes to bring them into the presence of Christ and remind them of the centrality of Christ to their beliefs.

We know that he was writing in some difficult circumstances, so his strategy is wise: he beckons the Corinthians to come back to the origins of their faith and sit at the feet of Christ.

In reminding the Corinthians about Christ, Paul did more than make them feel safe and accepted. He also reminded them what an amazing gift it is to receive faith in Christ (1 Corinthians 1:4). It is as a result of this gift, they had been enriched (1 Corinthians 1:5).

The word enriched is translated from the Greek word *ploutizo*, which refers to receiving great wealth. Paul uses it to describe the wealthy few, the plutocrats, who carried influence in any given community.

Imagine the impact of this phrase on the proud Greeks of Corinth, who already had elevated levels of self-importance due to their history of intellect and schools of philosophy. Paul tells them that they have been enriched in Christ. Even in their knowledge and speech, even in those areas where they already excelled, Christianity has brought them greater reasoning and understanding.

This additional understanding, this enrichment, wasn't a kind of secret knowledge they had to look for within themselves; rather, it was to be found in Christ (1 Corinthians 1:4). It was not earned, nor was it a reward. Enrichment was a gift, a blessing from the riches of Christ.

Paul gently reminds them that their lives have been potentiated. Christ has brought a fresh understanding to their perception of the world, enhancing their speech and reasoning through His gracious calling.

Paul goes on to explain that these blessings are complete, with no spiritual gift missing. They already had the ability to discern righteous from unrighteous behaviour, as well as the strength to pursue a holy life. Not only that, but the Corinthians would be supported in their calling through Jesus who would bring them faithfully to fellowship.

When we open mail, several clues alert us to the letter's content, including the colour of the envelope, the typesetting of the address label, or even the return address. Is it a bill? Perhaps a tax refund? Maybe it's a personal thank-you note or a newsletter.

Most ancient letters were secured with a wax seal. Some of these were personalized, but I don't suspect Paul had his own coat of arms to seal his parchments. Instead he used his introductions to do some of the work of the envelope—to set the tone through his choice of words and careful language.

Here in these opening verses, we see Christ. If there were an envelope window on this letter instead of a seal, we might see some imagery to depict the brilliance of Christ, perhaps gold leaf lettering or a gold leaf cross. We might also see the edge of a birthday card, for it's as if Paul wished to remind the Corinthians that on their birthday into Christianity they received a great gift of enrichment.

The message of these opening verses, the envelope window, is still relevant for us today. Despite our great advancements in reasoning and science, Christianity still enriches our speech and knowledge, just as it did for the ancient Greeks of Corinth.

APPLICATION: ENRICHED

- Take a moment to consider Paul's assertion that your life has been enriched through your belief in Christ.
- Read slowly through each verse and note Paul's deliberate inclusion of Jesus to underline his introductory statements. Let this lead you to give thanks for Christ. He is central and a common denominator for all Christians.
- Paul finishes his introduction by reminding the Corinthians that it's Christ's will for them to join Him in fellowship. Christ will work with them to accomplish this. Let Paul's thoughts remind you of Christ's desire for you to join Him both now and on that day.

What do we today, who no longer have any fear or awe of night, know of the great joy that our forefathers and the early Christians felt every morning at the return of light? If we were to learn again something of the praise and adoration that is due the triune God at the break of day, God the Father and Creator, who has preserved our life through the dark night and wakened us to a new day, God the Son and Saviour, who conquered death and hell for us and dwells in our midst as Victor, God the Holy Spirit who pours the bright gleam of God's Word into our hearts at the dawn of day, driving away all darkness and sin and teaching us to pray aright- then we would also begin to sense something of the joy that comes when night is past and brethren who dwell together in unity come together early in the morning for the common praise of their God, common hearing of the Word, and common prayer.[4]

—Dietrich Bonhoeffer

---

[4] Bonhoeffer, *Life Together*, 41.

Into Christ

1 CORINTHIANS 1:10–17

I appeal to you, brothers and sisters, in the name of our Lord Jesus Christ, that all of you agree with one another in what you say and that there be no divisions among you, but that you be perfectly united in mind and thought. [11] My brothers and sisters, some from Chloe's household have informed me that there are quarrels among you. [12] What I mean is this: One of you says, "I follow Paul"; another, "I follow Apollos"; another, "I follow Cephas"; still another, "I follow Christ."

[13] Is Christ divided? Was Paul crucified for you? Were you baptized in the name of Paul? [14] I thank God that I did not baptize any of you except Crispus and Gaius, [15] so no one can say that you were baptized in my name. [16] (Yes, I also baptized the household of Stephanas; beyond that, I don't remember if I baptized anyone else.) [17] For Christ did not send me to baptize, but to preach the gospel—not with wisdom and eloquence, lest the cross of Christ be emptied of its power.

Throughout 1 Corinthians, Paul writes about several disputes that had been brought to his attention. The first is mentioned here.

The people from Chloe's household are thought to have visited Corinth from Ephesus and returned to Paul with news of the Corinthian church. It was disturbing news, advising him that disunity had arisen in the church. The source of the disunity appeared to be misplaced loyalty; instead of focussing on Christ, some placed their loyalty primarily on faction leaders.

We can be sure that Apollos, Cephas, and Paul were true to the gospel. Therefore, any perceived differences in their messages had to have been manmade.

Paul continued to stress the centrality of Christ, reminding the Corinthians who it was they had been baptized into (1 Corinthians 1:14). Note that the Greek word *eis*, translated as "in," is a simple preposition. It could have more accurately been translated as "into," for this is the subtext of Paul's verse.

In the ancient world, oaths and property were sworn into a person's name to denote complete ownership and loyalty. For example, an officer of the Roman army was sworn into the name of Caesar. An adopted individual was sworn into the name of the family. A servant was given over into a family with complete abandonment of personal freedom.[5]

At a Christian baptism, we confess our loyalty to Christ, not to those performing the baptism or those who brought us to the

---

[5] William Barclay, *The New Daily Study Bible: The Letters to the Corinthians* (Louisville, KY: Westminster John Knox Press, 2002), 19.

point of conversion. No, our loyalty is into Christ. We are given over into His loyalty, His ownership.

Christ's governance of our lives fits well with the imagery of a soldier under a commanding officer, or perhaps a servant in a household. A Roman soldier did not drift in and out of the army. He committed to twenty-five years of loyal service. Similarly, we are not called to drift between our worldly works and those works of our Christian lives.

Joining the household of Christ is a full-time vocation, not a part-time gig. When we join, we enter completely. We don't leave parts of ourselves behind.

The soldier doesn't leave his hand or foot out of his allegiance to Caesar. The household servant is sworn over completely; nothing is left outside the house. For an adopted child, the whole being is given over, completely, simultaneously, and without holding anything back.

The concept of complete, unreserved, and eternal adoption into Christ is a starting point to achieving unity in the church.

Paul identifies how important this is by highlighting the significance of our baptism into Christ. He links unity with the concept of being baptized into Christ (1 Corinthians 1:13). In doing so, he uses a medical analogy. The Greek word translated as "perfectly unified" (1 Corinthians 1:11), *katertismenoi*, was commonly used to describe the perfect union of a broken bone.

Prior to our conversion, we were in need of healing; we were like broken bones. Spiritually, we were lost and without direction. Our progress through life was fractured. We were caught between our worldly desires and heavenly aspirations, just like the Corinthians.

Conversion and subsequent baptism reset our lives so we may be in union with Him and with one another. This produces a stronger alliance but requires us to acknowledge into whom we have been completely and eternally aligned.

Like the Corinthians, we need to be reminded that the nuances that separate our denominations are to be kept in their place. It is into Christ that we are baptized and aligned. He is the source of our unity. The rest of our differences must not be allowed to impair our vision of Him or distract our attention, lest we forget to whom we are to fix our gaze.

APPLICATION: INTO CHRIST

- It is a sobering thought that our baptism into Christ confesses an all-encompassing loyalty to Him. We are either all-in or not in at all. Renew your complete commitment to Jesus in prayer.
- Disunity is usually ugly, and occasionally it can't be avoided. In the midst of a dispute, we should be mindful of who it is we serve and be sure to walk graciously, remaining under His stewardship.
- Use the idea of realigning yourself to Christ in order to resolve a lack of unity and guide your prayers over matters of dispute.

Called

For the message of the cross is foolishness to those who are perishing, but to us who are being saved it is the power of God. ¹⁹ For it is written: "I will destroy the wisdom of the wise; the intelligence of the intelligent I will frustrate."

²⁰ Where is the wise person? Where is the teacher of the law? Where is the philosopher of this age? Has not God made foolish the wisdom of the world? ²¹ For since in the wisdom of God the world through its wisdom did not know him, God was pleased through the foolishness of what was preached to save those who believe. ²² Jews demand signs and Greeks look for wisdom, ²³ but we preach Christ crucified: a stumbling block to Jews and foolishness to Gentiles, ²⁴ but to those whom God has called, both Jews and Greeks, Christ the power of God and the wisdom of God. ²⁵ For the foolishness of God is wiser than human wisdom, and the weakness of God is stronger than human strength.

²⁶ Brothers and sisters, think of what you were when you were called. Not many of you were wise by human standards; not many were influential; not many were of

noble birth. [27] But God chose the foolish things of the world to shame the wise; God chose the weak things of the world to shame the strong. [28] God chose the lowly things of this world and the despised things—and the things that are not—to nullify the things that are, [29] so that no one may boast before him. [30] It is because of him that you are in Christ Jesus, who has become for us wisdom from God—that is, our righteousness, holiness and redemption. [31] Therefore, as it is written: "Let the one who boasts boast in the Lord."

[1] And so it was with me, brothers and sisters. When I came to you, I did not come with eloquence or human wisdom as I proclaimed to you the testimony about God. [2] For I resolved to know nothing while I was with you except Jesus Christ and him crucified. [3] I came to you in weakness with great fear and trembling. [4] My message and my preaching were not with wise and persuasive words, but with a demonstration of the Spirit's power, [5] so that your faith might not rest on human wisdom, but on God's power.

It has been said that the failure to recognize fine art is more a reflection of deficiencies in the observer than any lack of skill in the artist. A Rembrandt or da Vinci or Michelangelo piece should inspire the keen, discerning eye and be acknowledged for its brilliance. A lack of appreciation of such excellence suggests the eye is unseeing and the mind cold.

In the same way, the crucifixion of Christ is a litmus test.

Even as an impartial observer, it seems impossible not to be affected by the brutality of crucifixion. In the gospel accounts, we read that a Roman soldier who looked on wasn't immune to the tragedy. The terrible sight reached his battle-hardened heart and touched his humanity.

In the events of the cross, we observe the depraved cruelty of man to imagine and commit such a horrendous act. Crucifixion was abhorrent, an agonizing execution connived from an evil place in man's thoughts.

Contrast the man who could concoct such evil with one who is diametrically opposed. In the opposing corner of the human heart, we see an amazing act of sacrificial love. We see the unfathomable gift of grace.

Jesus found within His heart a gift of overwhelming generosity and mercy. He powerfully demonstrated the potential for man to be selfless beyond imagination. As fully human, He offered His life for the undeserving, exemplifying the amazing depths of love humanity can reach. This act of love stands in stark contrast to the act of torture to which He submitted.

At the cross, we see two sides of God. We observe in His Son the side we most want to appreciate, the side we like to hear and learn about: His amazing grace to take our place, suffer in our stead, and bring reconciliation.

God's other side, His righteous side, was also seen on the cross. His righteous justice demanded repayment for our unrighteousness. We are less keen on this side of God, though we cannot truthfully call it His worst side; it would be more fitting to call it His less popular side. This aspect of His character brings fear to our hearts that we might be exposed to the fullness of His judgment.

The reparations required for justice to be served were paid out unpleasantly, painfully, and in a grotesque manner. Such was the depth of those reparations. We don't like this righteous side of God. Understandably, we look at what happened to His Son and grow fearful.

This is like looking at fine art and failing to appreciate its beauty. To look on the cross and fail to see both the best and worst of mankind, as well as both sides of God, is to be heartless or numb. The cross must touch the heart, whether at a superficial human level, to see the depravity of man, or at the depth of the soul, from which we question where God was in these events.

If we aren't touched by the cross, there can be no life in our hearts. We are the unappreciative visitor who wanders an art gallery aimlessly, passing portraits and magnificent landscapes while ignoring the bold precision in these pieces and failing to comprehend their meaning. Such people are like the slumbering souls that Paul speaks of in His letters, describing those who haven't noticed God in the beauty of creation or not understood the message of the gospel.

But the Corinthians had responded. They were now children of the light, similar to the Thessalonians. The Holy Spirit had confirmed their saved status.

Sadly, the Corinthians had lost sight of the cross. They had forgotten what their eyes had seen when Paul preached the cross to them. He had taken them to the hill of Golgotha and deposited them at the foot of that hideous scaffold. They had beholden the best of man and experienced the unfathomable grace of God.

In that telling of the gospel, they had fallen on their knees and listened—and as they listened, they recognized. Their hearts felt something that had been forgotten. Their ears heard something they had stopped listening for. In the storytelling, in their imagining of the crucifixion events, they heard God's voice.

He called them not for their intellect, wealth, or status. He called them while they were figuratively at the cross, having been brought to that foolish place of desperate human cruelty. Even in those circumstances, God called them—and they heard. By listening, they perceived His desperate love, recognizing His lavish grace.

Paul reminded them that through the crucifixion God called both Jew and Gentile, for His power and wisdom were seen there (1 Corinthians 1:24).

If the Corinthians could listen again, they would hear God's voice as they came to the foot of the cross. That's where they needed to reside. That's where their redemption and acceptance could be found.

The cross and the call of God are central to our faith. Both are reminders that we haven't been saved by our righteous deeds or sanctimonious religion. We have been saved by His deeds and His call.

In reminding the Corinthians of the foundations of their salvation, Paul stripped away the misconceived idea that any one group had greater standing before God than the next. The playing field was level, and it was levelled by the cross and God's call.

APPLICATION: CALLED

- Knowing we have been called by God reassures us that we are loved and significant to Him. Thank God that He reached out to call you personally.
- God calls to us through different means, but certainly through the cross. Spending time before the figurative cross is a harrowing ordeal if we focus too much on its negative elements. I cannot imagine the suffering Christ experienced, but I do want to respond and give thanks for the grace and love we were selflessly given. I pray you will, too.
- In this letter, Paul takes the Corinthians back to the emotional experience of the cross to remind them of their need for God and His initiative to reach them. He reminds them to be humble in their faith and rely less on themselves and more on the wisdom of God. His words resonate in our current times; if we are prepared to listen, we will still benefit from God's call to be less self-absorbed and more cross-aware.

Freely Given

We do, however, speak a message of wisdom among the mature, but not the wisdom of this age or of the rulers of this age, who are coming to nothing. [7] No, we declare God's wisdom, a mystery that has been hidden and that God destined for our glory before time began. [8] None of the rulers of this age understood it, for if they had, they would not have crucified the Lord of glory. [9] However, as it is written: "What no eye has seen, what no ear has heard, and what no human mind has conceived"—the things God has prepared for those who love him—[10] these are the things God has revealed to us by his Spirit.

The Spirit searches all things, even the deep things of God. [11] For who knows a person's thoughts except their own spirit within them? In the same way no one knows the thoughts of God except the Spirit of God. [12] What we have received is not the spirit of the world, but the Spirit who is from God, so that we may understand what God has freely given us. [13] This is what we speak, not in words taught us by human wisdom but in words taught by the Spirit, explaining spiritual realities with Spirit-taught words. [14] The person without the Spirit does not accept the things that come from the Spirit of God but considers them foolishness, and cannot understand them because they are discerned only through the Spirit. [15] The person with the Spirit makes judgments about all things, but such a person is not subject to merely human judgments, [16] for, "Who has known the mind of the Lord so as to instruct him?" But we have the mind of Christ.

We learned in our previous reading that Paul preached the cross to demonstrate the depth and breadth of God's love and to highlight the fact that salvation is achieved not by our merits but by Christ. The Corinthians had glimpsed this purpose and begun to live as Christians.

But this was unsustainable for some who lost sight of the wisdom and power of the cross. For them, the value of Christ's act of salvation had depreciated, as if they became desensitized and forgot its poignancy. They reverted to being blind to the things of God.

In today's verses, Paul reiterates the importance of the cross and asserts how the cross is perceived: whether foolish or wise, weak or powerful, it has a profound effect on our faith. He also reminds the Corinthians that their view of the cross isn't solely under their governance but is deeply influenced by their willingness to hear the Holy Spirit.

There is a circular argument here, for we don't fully perceive the wisdom and power of the cross without the Spirit… but only through accepting the need for the cross do we receive the Spirit. It's as if our first glimpse of the cross captures our hearts; what convinces our minds is the insistence of the Holy Spirit.

The gift of the Holy Spirit is freely given, the Greek word for which is *charisthenta*, from the verb *charizomai*, which refers to grace or giving unmerited favour.

Although the English word charity has lost some its divine overtones, the original Greek conveys the idea that a gift is so magnanimous that it must have come from the gods. To these ancients, the Charities were mythological goddesses of charm, beauty, nature, and goodwill. They were the embodiment of kindness and benevolence.

By invoking memories of charity, Paul showed that the gifting of the Holy Spirit is a true blessing. In receiving the Holy Spirit, we are blessed to understand the glory of the cross.

Paul distinguishes between those who haven't received the Spirit and don't comprehend the cross and those who have received the Spirit and thus grasp the significance of Christ's crucifixion. In discussing the differences between these two groups, he comes to a staggering conclusion. By receiving the Holy Spirit, he had been gifted insight into the mind of Christ. You can almost imagine Paul pausing on this thought as it comes to him during the writing.

He implores the warring factions of the Corinthian church to look on the cross and be reminded of what lay behind this façade of cruelty. Without the cross, there could be no resurrection; without the cross, there could be no reconciliation; without the cross, there could be no Holy Spirit.

We understand therefore what lay behind the cross: the wisdom and power of God to mediate blessings and grant gifts to those who believe in Jesus. The gift of the Holy Spirit was given not according to prestige or intellect but through faith. This gift illuminated or magnified one's understanding of the cross, bringing about a change in perspective. This gift was none other than the spirit of He who had been on the cross.

As Christians, our spirit is reborn to be like His. Our thoughts are influenced by His thoughts; Our ways are diverted to merge with His. The cross therefore is a reminder of whose mind and spirit we have been gifted with.

Perhaps the subtitle for this passage should be The Eye of the Connoisseur. Through the blessing of the Holy Spirit, we, like the Corinthians, see the cross differently. As we view the cross through the gift of the mind of Christ, we ought not to shy away from looking on. Rather, we should feel His blessing, for it is a beautiful reminder of His power and wisdom, but mostly His grace.

APPLICATION: FREELY GIVEN

- The reason for Paul's letter was the development of factions within the church. To find common ground among them, he skillfully but aptly reminds them to whom they ought to align themselves. Being still before the cross is a great way to find peace, whether it's from everyday hustle and bustle or the minefields of conflict.

- Paul's conclusion that we have been given the mind of Christ is an extraordinary way to explain the gift of the Holy Spirit. Take a moment to think on this perspective. It's not one that is commonly used to describe the Holy Spirit. Paul's imagery emphasizes the power of the cross to deliver such a gift.
- Paul writes that the Spirit teaches. It's not a one-time-only present that brings instant enlightenment. Consider your approach to learning from the Spirit and whether you remain open to His lessons.

Grow

Brothers and sisters, I could not address you as people who live by the Spirit but as people who are still worldly—mere infants in Christ. ² I gave you milk, not solid food, for you were not yet ready for it. Indeed, you are still not ready. ³ You are still worldly. For since there is jealousy and quarreling among you, are you not worldly? Are you not acting like mere humans? ⁴ For when one says, "I follow Paul," and another, "I follow Apollos," are you not mere human beings?

⁵ What, after all, is Apollos? And what is Paul? Only servants, through whom you came to believe—as the Lord has assigned to each his task. ⁶ I planted the seed, Apollos watered it, but God has been making it grow. ⁷ So neither the one who plants nor the one who waters is anything, but only God, who makes things grow. ⁸ The one who plants and the one who waters have one purpose, and they will each be rewarded according to their own labor. ⁹ For we are co-workers in God's service; you are God's field, God's building.

¹⁰ By the grace God has given me, I laid a foundation as a wise builder, and someone else is building on

it. But each one should build with care. [11] For no one can lay any foundation other than the one already laid, which is Jesus Christ. [12] If anyone builds on this foundation using gold, silver, costly stones, wood, hay or straw, [13] their work will be shown for what it is, because the Day will bring it to light. It will be revealed with fire, and the fire will test the quality of each person's work. [14] If what has been built survives, the builder will receive a reward. [15] If it is burned up, the builder will suffer loss but yet will be saved—even though only as one escaping through the flames.

[16] Don't you know that you yourselves are God's temple and that God's Spirit dwells in your midst? [17] If anyone destroys God's temple, God will destroy that person; for God's temple is sacred, and you together are that temple.

[18] Do not deceive yourselves. If any of you think you are wise by the standards of this age, you should become "fools" so that you may become wise. [19] For the wisdom of this world is foolishness in God's sight. As it is written: "He catches the wise in their craftiness"; [20] and again, "The Lord knows that the thoughts of the wise are futile." [21] So then, no more boasting about human leaders! All things are yours, [22] whether Paul or Apollos or Cephas or the world or life or death or the present or the future—all are yours, [23] and you are of Christ, and Christ is of God.

Paul is trying to dissolve the fractious factions that arose in Corinth as a result of the people placing too much emphasis on nuances between Apollos, Paul, and Cephas. He addresses this by having the Corinthians refocus their attention on the cross and away from eloquence and worldly wisdom. He stresses the importance of allowing the Holy Spirit to lead them as they seek to understand more of the wisdom and power of the cross. Finally, he challenges them to mature in their belief, since their squabbles reveal their undeveloped spirituality.

Paul, Apollos, and Cephas each had roles to play in bringing the gospel to the Corinthians. Paul acknowledges that if he planted the seed and Apollos watered it, God made it grow (1 Corinthians 3:6–7). And therein lay the problem for the arguing Corinthians: they had forgotten the central role of God, the vital ingredient for their spiritual development.

A seed can be planted and a shoot can be watered, but it won't grow unless it's placed in the light. The shoot needs to be fed sunlight to develop and grow. Without the energy from the sun, the plant will remain a shoot. It won't bear fruit or grow to a sufficient stature to withstand inclement weather. It may wither.

The fractious Christian needs to spend more time in the light, in front of the cross, being humbled by the grace of Christ and awed by His sacrifice. Our points of contention dissolve when we see them in the context of the glorious gift we have been bestowed.

The cross has the ability to resolve conflicts between Christians. This is part of the crucifixion's inherent wisdom. This gift can be ours if we are willing to submit to what we see there.

The word for growth in 1 Corinthians 3:6 and 7 comes from *auxano*, which can be translated as "to make grow, to increase."

Spiritual maturity, growth in our understanding and acceptance of Christ, is achieved through God's blessing. If we are unavailable to receive God's blessing, He cannot deliver it and we will fail to grow. If we aren't exposed to sufficient light, if we choose to remain in the dark, our growth will be stunted.

Spiritual maturity isn't gained through an intellectual exercise or aesthetic practice. It's a gift of grace, much like the cross, and is naturally obtained by seeking God with a humble, open heart.

We have adopted the Greek word *auxano* into English as auxin, which is the name we use for the growth hormone that causes a plant to grow from its tip. Without this hormone, the shoot doesn't grow upward toward the light and fails to develop.

Much like a plant growing towards the sun under the influence of auxin, we grow towards the nature of the Father under the influence of the Holy Spirit. This analogy highlights the passive nature of spiritual growth; our role, and therefore the role of the Corinthians, is to be present before God.

In 1 Corinthians 3:15–16, Paul addresses the natural question that arises when Christians don't mature: is their salvation secure? To answer it, Paul paints the picture of someone who runs from a blazing home. Salvation is possible, but with a fine margin for success.

My sense is that the question of whether perpetual sinners can be saved comes from a worldly heart. A better question would be to ask this: why would a person not be so moved by the cross that their natural instinct wouldn't be to spend time in the light, to desire the light, like a shoot does the sun?

Our responsibility, like for the Corinthians, is to come into the light and be matured by His grace, His auxin. We shouldn't seek to play in the shadows but take our place in His garden.

APPLICATION: GROW

- As Christians, we devote a lot of time to trying to grow. This endeavour comes from well-meaning motives. In our endeavours, let us reflect to ensure we're open to receiving the lessons He would pass on. We should be more like the young plant that passively receives sunlight.
- If growth is obtained by being with the Lord, spend a few moments figuratively before the cross, giving thanks and feeling blessed.
- I'm not sure how we should measure our own spiritual maturity. We can reflect on how our views and behaviours have changed to become more in keeping with our heavenly home. Give thanks to God for this development and ask that He would continue to pour His light into your life.

Faithful

This, then, is how you ought to regard us: as servants of Christ and as those entrusted with the mysteries God has revealed. [2] Now it is required that those who have been given a trust must prove faithful. [3] I care very little if I am judged by you or by any human court; indeed, I do not even judge myself. [4] My conscience is clear, but that does not make me innocent. It is the Lord who judges me. [5] Therefore judge nothing before the appointed time; wait until the Lord comes. He will bring to light what is hidden in darkness and will expose the motives of the heart. At that time each will receive their praise from God.

[6] Now, brothers and sisters, I have applied these things to myself and Apollos for your benefit, so that you may learn from us the meaning of the saying, "Do not go beyond what is written." Then you will not be puffed up in being a follower of one of us over against the other. [7] For who makes you different from anyone else? What do you have that you did not receive? And if you did receive it, why do you boast as though you did not?

[8] Already you have all you want! Already you have become rich! You have begun to reign—and that without us! How I wish that you really had begun to reign so that we also might reign with you! [9] For it seems to me that God has put us apostles on display at the end of the procession, like those condemned to die in the arena. We have been made a spectacle to the whole universe, to angels as well as to human beings. [10] We are fools for Christ, but you are so wise in Christ! We are weak, but you are strong! You are honored, we are dishonored! [11] To this very hour we go hungry and thirsty, we are in rags, we are brutally treated, we are homeless. [12] We work hard with our own hands. When we are cursed, we bless; when we are persecuted, we endure it; [13] when we are slandered, we answer kindly. We have become the scum of the earth, the garbage of the world—right up to this moment.

[14] I am writing this not to shame you but to warn you as my dear children. [15] Even if you had ten thousand guardians in Christ, you do not have many fathers, for in Christ Jesus I became your father through the gospel. [16] Therefore I urge you to imitate me. [17] For this reason I have sent to you Timothy, my son whom I love, who is faithful in the Lord. He will remind you of my way of life in Christ Jesus, which agrees with what I teach everywhere in every church.

[18] Some of you have become arrogant, as if I were not coming to you. [19] But I will come to you very soon,

if the Lord is willing, and then I will find out not only how these arrogant people are talking, but what power they have. [20] For the kingdom of God is not a matter of talk but of power. [21] What do you prefer? Shall I come to you with a rod of discipline, or shall I come in love and with a gentle spirit?

In this passage, Paul moves through the gears of rhetorical styles to emphasize the importance of his argument. He calls the Corinthians to attention. He tries to turn their heads and engage them. He reminds them of the message of the cross and the voices of their teachers.

Like the sun rising on a misty fall morning, he aims to burn off the morning dew to enable them to see again with clarity what they first believed and from whom they were taught it. If they are able to glimpse these beliefs through the fog of worldly influence, Paul hopes they may return to pursuing the things of Christ, to pursuing maturity in their belief.

He addresses the arrogance of some in the Corinthian church who assume an authority in excess of those who brought the gospel. This reveals a lack of humility. Their self-justification undermines their claims to spiritual maturity.

As he winds up this part of his message, Paul drifts into some emotional rhetoric (1 Corinthians 4:8–13). Hidden amongst these verses, and acting as bookends to the passage, is an appeal to emulate or imitate the trustworthiness of faithful Paul (1 Corinthians 4:2, 16). His comments beg the question of what is faithful behaviour in Christian terms.

The Greek word used by Paul for the word faithful in 1 Corinthians 4:2 is *pisto*, derived from *pietho*, which means "to believe or have confidence in, or to be trustworthy." Paul makes the point in 1 Corinthians 4:1 that as a Christian he was privileged to have the mystery of Christ unveiled. He was entrusted with an understanding of it. Having been given this trust, it is his duty to demonstrate that he is indeed trustworthy.

Some of the Corinthians displayed unfaithfulness. They weren't trusting the message they had been taught and which they had confessed to believe. They had lost sight of the preciousness of the grace that had been bestowed upon them through the cross.

Their self-justification revealed that they didn't perceive how lowly their position had been before their restoration. Neither did they respect who had restored them or understand how they had been restored. Christ, not their self-justification, had pulled them up from the foot of the cross and made them stand.

The motivation to remain faithful to and mindful of whom we owe our fealty comes from a deep appreciation of what has been bestowed on us through the cross. By pursuing maturity and sanctification, we are not seeking to gain more of Christ's favour, nor does He require our compliance. That would mean our salvation is influenced by works, rendering His suffering insufficient.

Paul's appeal to remain trustworthy is simply a reminder of something we as Christians feel drawn to at our conversion and may later forget: our natural desire to remain faithful, having appreciated the grace of Christ. Sometimes we need to be reminded of His grace to be more adherent in our faithfulness.

This is what Paul reminds the Corinthians about. He extolls them to be mature and not quarrelsome, to be respectful and not arrogant, to not be presumptuous in their understanding but to rather be mindful of their teachers. In these matters, he desired that they would demonstrate faithfulness or trustworthiness to the precious message they had been given to understand.

The revelation of who Jesus was is a gift in and of itself. When we appreciate this, our perspective shifts, generating a response of gratitude. Our appreciation should then manifest in our behaviour.

Paul calls on the Corinthians to be reminded of their belief and act appropriately in a manner that shows they are faithful to the trust that has been bestowed upon them.

As modern readers, here is the challenge. We may not have drifted as far as some among the Corinthians did, but we are also prone to forget how to appropriately respond to the faith we have been given.

APPLICATION: FAITHFUL

- Thank God for the blessing of recognizing Jesus, for it is a gift. Pray that you would be faithful and trustworthy with the gift.
- Consider what it could mean for you to demonstrate your trustworthiness. Any response should be natural and not performance-related. Just as we delight in delicious food, we should delight in being trustworthy in demonstrating Christian maturity.

Faithful: 1 Corinthians 4:1-21

- Think of examples of faithfulness, whether it's a close friend, work colleague, or even a pet. What aspects of their behaviour reassure you of their trustworthiness? Let these examples prompt your prayers as to how you can demonstrate your faithfulness to Christ.

Unleavened

1 CORINTHIANS 5:1–13

It is actually reported that there is sexual immorality among you, and of a kind that even pagans do not tolerate: A man is sleeping with his father's wife. [2] And you are proud! Shouldn't you rather have gone into mourning and have put out of your fellowship the man who has been doing this? [3] For my part, even though I am not physically present, I am with you in spirit. As one who is present with you in this way, I have already passed judgment in the name of our Lord Jesus on the one who has been doing this. [4] So when you are assembled and I am with you in spirit, and the power of our Lord Jesus is present, [5] hand this man over to Satan for the destruction of the flesh, so that his spirit may be saved on the day of the Lord.

[6] Your boasting is not good. Don't you know that a little yeast leavens the whole batch of dough? [7] Get rid of the old yeast, so that you may be a new unleavened batch—as you really are. For Christ, our Passover lamb, has been sacrificed. [8] Therefore let us keep the Festival, not with the old bread leavened with malice and wick-

edness, but with the unleavened bread of sincerity and truth.

[9] I wrote to you in my letter not to associate with sexually immoral people—[10] not at all meaning the people of this world who are immoral, or the greedy and swindlers, or idolaters. In that case you would have to leave this world. [11] But now I am writing to you that you must not associate with anyone who claims to be a brother or sister but is sexually immoral or greedy, an idolater or slanderer, a drunkard or swindler. Do not even eat with such people.

[12] What business is it of mine to judge those outside the church? Are you not to judge those inside? [13] God will judge those outside. "Expel the wicked person from among you."

In this book's introduction, I remarked that Paul left a wake after his time in Corinth. He brought the gospel, the news of God's remarkable visit to the earth in the form of Jesus, a message that had the ability to clear away the choppy waters of the people's old lives and take them in a new direction.

Upon reading today's passage, it seems that some members of the congregation had clung to aspects of their old lives. Despite the opportunity to experience Eden in the wake of receiving the gospel, some chose to return to the desert—a desert characterized by wretched behaviour.

To a Christian, there can be no greater desire than to please God and keep His word. We learn of this in Ecclesiastes 12:13:

"Now all has been heard; here is the conclusion of the matter: fear God and keep his commandments, for this is the duty of all mankind." If this dictum is to be upheld, there can be no boasting (1 Corinthians 5:2) about a flagrant rebellion against one of God's laws (Leviticus 18:8). According to Leviticus, it was unlawful for a man to be in a relationship with his stepmother.

Most readers today would be horrified of such an act being upheld or boasted of in the Corinthian congregation. We would find such an impropriety distasteful, shameful, and utterly abhorrent.

The Greco-Roman culture was different from that of the Jews, and some in the Corinthian church may have been oblivious to the guidance found in Leviticus. Similarly, the Greco-Roman culture was different from ours. Therefore, we can't assume that the Corinthians had the same moral standards.

Some aspects of that Greco-Roman culture are transferrable to our own today. Self-expression and individualism were popular then and remain so now. In modern Western societies, the rights of individuals have replaced the moral frameworks found in God's word. So for the secular world of the twenty-first century, the sin of 1 Corinthians 5:1 would be acceptable, provided that both parties consented as individuals.

From a biblical perspective, the sin was abhorrent. But it was the lack of insight into the depravity of the sin and its unholiness that seems to have provoked Paul. Pursuing such an act meant ignoring the new spiritual birth that occurred at conversion.

In these verses, we see a challenge to the Corinthian church. It was a corporate challenge, but we should make it a personal one. Paul encouraged the Corinthians to be *unleavened* (1 Corinthians 5:7).

The leaven is a batch of dough with yeast that has been fermented and used as a rising agent in a new loaf. Unleavened bread doesn't use the old dough, however; it is made from new ingredients. The call to be like unleavened bread is therefore a call to be pure and untainted by our lives prior to becoming Christians.

Unleavened bread had a special place in Jewish culture, as it was the bread they were instructed to make in haste as they left Egypt. They left in a hurry and had no time to allow the bread to rise. This became a symbol of their God-given freedom (Deuteronomy 16:3).

Paul speaks of unleavened bread rather than reiterating his call for the people to return to the cross, which had been his approach in 1 Corinthians 1–4. The symbolism of unleavened bread serves as an alternative reminder of the salvation story.

Paul wanted the Corinthians to see a correlation between unleavened bread and the cross. For the Corinthians, the comparison would have presented a stark contrast. It was supposed to make them sit up and take notice, to stir them from complacency and remind them who they were and what they had become.

For us today, unleavened bread isn't particularly relevant as a metaphor. However, we might think of Paul's illustration when we see an ordinary loaf of bread. To draw comparisons between a loaf of bread and the cross is belittling to the cross, but Paul's aim was to jar us. The bread reminds us *who* made us rise again to a new life, washed, purified, and elevated to do good works.

APPLICATION: UNLEAVENED

- We aren't likely to come across unleavened bread in our day-to-day lives, so why not use the imagery of a regular loaf to remind you of the call to be purified in Christ?
- When we smell fresh bread baking in the oven, it has a pleasing aroma. This is the kind of Christianity we hope to be known for—pleasing, pure, and rich in grace. Pray that God would help you identify any unpleasant behaviours that might be spoiling your freshly baked smell.
- At the core of the problem in 1 Corinthians 5 is the elevation of the self to be more important than God's law. Self is the leaven that can spoil our relationship with Christ. When you're next enjoying your toast, sandwich, roll, or wrap, think about ways in which you might promote Christ's choices for your life rather than your own.

Washed Away

If any of you has a dispute with another, do you dare to take it before the ungodly for judgment instead of before the Lord's people? [2] Or do you not know that the Lord's people will judge the world? And if you are to judge the world, are you not competent to judge trivial cases? [3] Do you not know that we will judge angels? How much more the things of this life! [4] Therefore, if you have disputes about such matters, do you ask for a ruling from those whose way of life is scorned in the church? [5] I say this to shame you. Is it possible that there is nobody among you wise enough to judge a dispute between believers? [6] But instead, one brother takes another to court—and this in front of unbelievers!

[7] The very fact that you have lawsuits among you means you have been completely defeated already. Why not rather be wronged? Why not rather be cheated? [8] Instead, you yourselves cheat and do wrong, and you do this to your brothers and sisters. [9] Or do you not know that wrongdoers will not inherit the kingdom of God? Do not be deceived: Neither the sexually immoral nor idolaters nor adulterers nor men who have sex with men

[10] nor thieves nor the greedy nor drunkards nor slanderers nor swindlers will inherit the kingdom of God. [11] And that is what some of you were. But you were washed, you were sanctified, you were justified in the name of the Lord Jesus Christ and by the Spirit of our God.

Are there issues you come across that provoke you to passionate anger? I'm not suggesting these issues might cause you to express that anger; rather, there are certain concerns that raise your hackles when you experience them. For parents, this type of response is expected when a child is at risk of harm. In such circumstances, Dad or Mom want to console their child. But we also expect them to get angry, or at least express displeasure in a strong, no-nonsense manner at whoever hurt their child.

The same type of visceral response is often provoked when we experience injustice, whether it's directed at us or others with whom we empathize. We feel an emotional drive to see justice prevail.

These common experiences can produce unpleasant mob behaviours, or even radicalization.

A more frequent example is the sense of injustice that leads people to feel road rage. The offended driver feels compelled to "educate" a fellow driver of appropriate road etiquette.

In today's passage, Paul discusses how this desire for justice among Christians can make us come across as too hungry or pedantic. In our obsessiveness, we can paint the church in a poor light. He gives us an opportunity not only to reflect on our disputes but to ask about the purpose of church.

He suggests, for example, that the church can act as a court of law to help resolve minor issues between members of the congregation.

Multiple roles have been described for the church, prominent among them teaching, instructing in God's word, worshipping God, and fellowshipping with other believers. The latter role is pertinent to today's reading, for it is difficult to be in fellowship and dispute with a brother (Matthew 5:23–25).

As we mature as Christians, it might be argued that the roles of worshipping and fellowshipping are even more important. There are fewer and fewer places where we are able to meet as Christians and share our experiences of God. Trying to explain our experiences—being with Christ, feeling the influence of the Holy Spirit, or recognizing the sound of God's voice—can be a bit like trying to explain the taste and texture of ice cream to someone who has never experienced it. The cold, soft, sweetness, and crunchy-yet-smooth consistency may be beyond their experience, and possibly their imagination. All we can offer the naïve are poor similes that in no way substitute for the real Haagen-Dazs or Ben and Jerry's experience.

We attend church, or at least I hope we do, to have the opportunity to share and speak about our experiences with God. We go to meet like-minded people and relate to them about our kingdom thoughts and desires. We feel the preciousness of fellowship in addition to the fundamental truth that we are meeting in God's house, and it's becoming rarer as our society increasingly turns away from Christianity.

Paul exhorts the Corinthians to protect the environment of the church and treat the church with a precious, caring attitude. The church in Corinth was just starting up. As such, there were few places where Christians could meet, worship, and fellowship.

He also advises these Christians to be mindful that their passion for justice doesn't lead to a stain on the church's reputation. Paul's words may be challenging for those who have experienced the passionate emotions of injustice. It's not so simple to give up a firmly held position.

In 1 Corinthians 6:11, Paul appeals to the Corinthians to remember the preciousness of their Christian experience. He reminds them they have been washed, and the word Paul chooses is *apolouo*. Implicit in this word are two concepts: firstly, something has been washed away, and secondly, it's a passive event. In other words, these Corinthian Christians allowed themselves to be washed.

Paul didn't use *baptizo*, which might have stressed the spiritual renewal. Instead he was emphasizing that they were completely purified, the mind, body, and soul having been washed clean. As such, it was time for them to be reconciled.

If they failed to understand their new purity, their *apolouo* was incomplete and Jesus's work had been insufficient.

In life, as in chess, it's hard to give up our pawns. They sometimes occupy key spaces on the board, holding the fort on important avenues, controlling territories, and influencing other pieces. Yet we wouldn't sacrifice the king or another major piece for a pawn. That would be foolish.

We need to be mindful that we don't fall into a similar spiritual trap. Let's not pursue righteousness for righteousness' sake at the expense of He who washed us.

APPLICATION: WASHED AWAY

- In the heat of the moment, it can be difficult to hold on to platitudes such as "Just let it wash away." If your sense of injustice occasionally gets the better of you, use some of the analogies we've considered above to help cool off.
- Pray for insight into situations where you continue to hold onto injustice. Ask God for the wisdom to know how to wash it away.
- If you do have grievances or perceived hurts related to other church members, you may find reconciliation through conversations with trusted confidants. In these situations, proving you're right ought to come second to achieving reconciliation. Wise counsel may help to determine how best to wash away your own agenda to adopt His.

Glued

"I have the right to do anything," you say—but not everything is beneficial. "I have the right to do anything"—but I will not be mastered by anything. ¹³ You say, "Food for the stomach and the stomach for food, and God will destroy them both." The body, however, is not meant for sexual immorality but for the Lord, and the Lord for the body. ¹⁴ By his power God raised the Lord from the dead, and he will raise us also. ¹⁵ Do you not know that your bodies are members of Christ himself? Shall I then take the members of Christ and unite them with a prostitute? Never! ¹⁶ Do you not know that he who unites himself with a prostitute is one with her in body? For it is said, "The two will become one flesh." ¹⁷ But whoever is united with the Lord is one with him in spirit.

¹⁸ Flee from sexual immorality. All other sins a person commits are outside the body, but whoever sins sexually, sins against their own body. ¹⁹ Do you not know that your bodies are temples of the Holy Spirit, who is in you, whom you have received from God? You

are not your own; [20] you were bought at a price. Therefore, honor God with your bodies.

Today's passage includes some socially awkward verses. It's
becoming clearer why 1 Corinthians isn't a regular Sunday
morning feature in churches that lean on expository book-by-
book, verse-by-verse preaching. Sex remains a taboo topic for
both preaching and polite dinner conversation.

Much like injustice, one's thoughts and behaviours associated with sex generate passionate feelings. And just like those
emotions associated with righteous indignation, sexual thoughts
and behaviours need to be controlled by Christians if the church's
reputation is to be maintained.

We understood from 1 Corinthians 6:1–11 that it's harmful
to the church if members argue amongst themselves or go to court
rather than settle matters internally. We observed that the church
is a precious organization that offers fellowship found nowhere
else. As such, church members have a duty, privilege, and interest
in maintaining fellowship rather than pursuing arbitrary disputes.
We also learned the value of sacrificing a pawn to spare the queen
or letting go of righteous indignation for the sake of the king.

First Corinthians 6:12–20 explores similar instinctive emotional drives that if given full freedom could undermine the reputation of the church. Although the target of these drives seems to
be people outside the church body, the effects of such behaviour
are still impactful.

Upon becoming a Christian, a person's worldview funda-
mentally changes. Whether we're aware of it or not, secular people

are led by a philosophy that denies the existence of God and only values man's values. Secular law leaves no room for a reflection of God's values.

At Christian conversion, or during sanctification, an individual turns toward God and away from a philosophy that idealizes human thought and understands that human behaviour, left unchecked, leads naturally away from God.

The Christian holds to the fact that man is fallen and will instinctively err from God's ways. New Christians enter a new magnetic field whose pull is toward God and holiness, away from secularism and relativism.

It's not solely an academic exercise to understand the shift in our so-called magnetic polarity. It's relevant to the passage, too, for Paul is concerned that some in the Corinthian congregation were aligning with a polarity that pulled them away from Christianity.

Paul uses secular phrases, denoted with quotation marks, to challenge the behaviour of some in the Corinthian church. They had continued to celebrate their humanity by conforming to the cultural expectations of the day.

He also uses colloquial rhetoric to appeal to the people's colloquial behaviour, highlighting why their promiscuity was so damaging. On a relationship level, the damage is obvious: marriages destroyed, wrecked families, irreparable friendships, and destroyed trust.

However, there's a deeper destructive influence from choosing to embrace the world's view on sex, and it's felt on an individual level.

We are left to contemplate what Paul was driving at in 1 Corinthians 6:18, which implies a unique element to promiscuity that makes it deeply offensive to God and deeply damaging to ourselves. If we could understand this, we might be better armed against temptation.

One thought is that the word for body, *soma*, in 1 Corinthians 6:18–20 is representative of not just flesh (*sarx*) but of the whole person—mind, body, and soul. This would be in keeping with the concept in 1 Corinthians 6:15–17 that sex isn't simply a physical act; it involves spiritual (soul) and emotional (mind) connection.

The word united in 1 Corinthians 6:15–17 is translated from, *kollomenos*, which is derived from *kollao*, referring to something that is glued together or connected with another. It's the same word used to describe marriage in Matthew 19:5, and it references Genesis 2:24.

Sex was never intended to be a casual act. Such a lack of commitment denies the reality of the intimate connection. Casual sex denies the existence of a lasting bond between couples. Extramarital sex denies how painful the behaviour is for the innocent spouse. It pulls on the marriage glue, offending mind, body, and soul. Like peeling apart fibres of Velcro, sexual promiscuity pulls us away from each other, and from Christ, taking us toward the abyss of secular morality.

Paul stressed that sex, as a physical link between individuals, is similar in character to that which binds us to Christ at conversion. We are glued mind, body, and soul to Christ.

In this light, the misdemeanours of some in the congregation no longer seem innocuous. These Corinthians ignored a change in the magnetic polarity that should point to God. Through casual sex, they risked personal and spiritual ruin.

Like the Corinthians, we should strive for more *kollao*—stronger glue to fix ourselves to Christ and our spouses. Honouring God with our bodies isn't just a call to honour one another with our flesh, but also with our minds and souls. This type of honour requires us not to interfere with His magnetic pull, so we will be readily aligned to His will.

APPLICATION: GLUED

- The grace of Jesus will cover, and does cover, all our sins—past, present, and future. He is able to heal past sexual sin and bring peace. Times of reflection are important in helping us refresh our bonds to Him.
- Biblical attitudes toward promiscuity aren't celebrated in Western society. We may struggle to convince new Christians of the eternal validity of the values Paul imposed on the Corinthians. Pray that nothing would interfere with the magnetic pull toward Christ in those you know who may be struggling with these issues.
- Pray for wisdom to avoid situations that might lead to sexual transgressions, whether it be by avoiding the internet, certain movies, or social circumstances.

Authority

Now for the matters you wrote about: "It is good for a man not to have sexual relations with a woman." [2] But since sexual immorality is occurring, each man should have sexual relations with his own wife, and each woman with her own husband. [3] The husband should fulfill his marital duty to his wife, and likewise the wife to her husband. [4] The wife does not have authority over her own body but yields it to her husband. In the same way, the husband does not have authority over his own body but yields it to his wife. [5] Do not deprive each other except perhaps by mutual consent and for a time, so that you may devote yourselves to prayer. Then come together again so that Satan will not tempt you because of your lack of self-control. [6] I say this as a concession, not as a command. [7] I wish that all of you were as I am. But each of you has your own gift from God; one has this gift, another has that.

[8] Now to the unmarried and the widows I say: It is good for them to stay unmarried, as I do. [9] But if they cannot control themselves, they should marry, for it is better to marry than to burn with passion.

¹⁰ To the married I give this command (not I, but the Lord): A wife must not separate from her husband. ¹¹ But if she does, she must remain unmarried or else be reconciled to her husband. And a husband must not divorce his wife.

¹² To the rest I say this (I, not the Lord): If any brother has a wife who is not a believer and she is willing to live with him, he must not divorce her. ¹³ And if a woman has a husband who is not a believer and he is willing to live with her, she must not divorce him. ¹⁴ For the unbelieving husband has been sanctified through his wife, and the unbelieving wife has been sanctified through her believing husband. Otherwise your children would be unclean, but as it is, they are holy.

¹⁵ But if the unbeliever leaves, let it be so. The brother or the sister is not bound in such circumstances; God has called us to live in peace. ¹⁶ How do you know, wife, whether you will save your husband? Or, how do you know, husband, whether you will save your wife?

Before we married, my wife and I were blessed to know godly Christians. They recommended we take the commitment to marriage seriously and invest time in a pre-marriage course. These types of courses are often run by missionary or evangelical organizations. The one we attended was run by the Navigators. It was an opportunity for us to spend a weekend together, away from other pressures, and talk through the topics our course guides recommended.

I remember discussing our families and relationships with each other's parents. We were encouraged to reflect on potential baggage we might bring into our new relationship, whether from our own past or how we'd seen our parents interact. I think we might have touched on the physical aspects of our relationship, but I don't recall any conversions like the one Paul wrote about in this passage.

The closest we came to receiving such advice was after our engagement when our friends gave us each a copy of Joyce Huggett's *Two into One*.[6] We agreed not to read Chapter Nine, entitled "Sex: The Good News," until after we were married.

Perhaps Paul would have recommended we read it ahead of time. I suspect he would have approved of its content, since he wrote 1 Corinthians 7:1–16 in response to questions the earnest Corinthians had asked.

Corinth, with its licentious culture, had developed some unhelpful views on physical relationships. Christianity had challenged these views. Some in the Corinthian congregation had begun to develop their own ideas as to how best to demonstrate their commitment to God by rejecting their prior lives and practices.

Into this backdrop, Paul offers some practical advice. We read with interest how he explores the difficult scenarios faced by young Corinthian Christians. He hangs his framework on certain foundational truths, granting credibility and acceptance to the

---

[6] Joyce Huggett, *Two into One* (Leicester, UK: Intervarsity Press, 1993).

single and married, the widowed and widowers. He even address-es married Christians whose spouses may not believe. In this, he expresses Christ's attitude to be gracious to all and non-dismis-sive, no matter the circumstances.

As he did in 1 Corinthians 6, Paul writes that an appropriate view of our bodies includes meaningful reflection on how our per-spective changes after conversion.

It is true we don't have the perfect resurrection bodies we hope to receive in heaven, the ones without pain, infirmity, or dis-ability. We do, however, host the Holy Spirit, whose help increas-es our awareness of our propensity to be sinful if left to our own devices.

We can no longer subscribe to the romantic notion that we express true authenticity in our humanity. Instead we hear Paul's words: *"You are not your own; you were bought at a price. Therefore honour God with your bodies"* (1 Corinthians 6:19–20).

Paul applies this idea of handing over authority and own-ership of our bodies to the marriage relationship (1 Corinthians 7:4). Each partner has authority over the other. This isn't a carte blanche for abuse, oppression, or exploitation; it is simply an extension of our altered understanding of our position and phi-losophy, for we are now no longer our own bosses, married or oth-erwise. We instead place ourselves under Christ's authority.

The word Paul uses for authority is *exousiazo*, which conveys the notion of having the right and power to preside over another. This idea, that we should submit ourselves to another, is unworld-ly but speaks to our wish to align and submit ourselves to the authority of Jesus.

Neither exercise is easy, whether submitting to the Lord or to our spouse. Giving up control runs contrary to our innate human drive to be independent.

When we think of submitting to Christ, we remember Matthew 16:24 and strive to obey: *"Then Jesus said to his disciples, 'Whoever wants to be my disciple must deny themselves and take up their cross and follow me.'"* This is surely the key to adhering to Paul's advice in marriage. In our new Christian bodies, with the Holy Spirit inside us and our awareness of sin, we are to be selfless in our pursuit of Christ-centeredness. In our Christ-centeredness, we will be able to accede to the wishes of our spouses.

Paul offers various scenarios in his letter. The key for the Corinthians, he writes, is for them to go from being self-seeking to Christ-seeking, striving to serve others. This remains our challenge in relationships today.

When presented with the idea of yielding our authority to another, we tread very carefully, hoping that our imprint doesn't weigh heavily on them. We step as though we're dancers, not foot soldiers.

For me, this is what the phrase "two into one" is all about: playing a piece of music together on different instruments. By accompanying each other, we are able to express the tune with a togetherness that wouldn't be possible were we to perform alone. In marriage, our harmonizing notes complement each other.

APPLICATION: AUTHORITY

- Consider again Paul's words in Corinthians 6:19–20. How does it make you feel to know that you have responsibilities to Christ with your body?
- If married, Paul says you have bodily responsibilities to your spouse. Pray about this and consider your attitude to your spouse in this regard.
- Paul doesn't condemn marriage or singleness, nor does he condemn marriages of mixed faith. Pray for those you know who find themselves in challenging situations, whether married or unmarried. Ask that they would be aware of God's blessing no matter their circumstances.

Freed Person

1 CORINTHIANS 7:17–24

Nevertheless, each person should live as a believer in whatever situation the Lord has assigned to them, just as God has called them. This is the rule I lay down in all the churches. ¹⁸ Was a man already circumcised when he was called? He should not become uncircumcised. Was a man uncircumcised when he was called? He should not be circumcised. ¹⁹ Circumcision is nothing and uncircumcision is nothing. Keeping God's commands is what counts. ²⁰ Each person should remain in the situation they were in when God called them.

²¹ Were you a slave when you were called? Don't let it trouble you—although if you can gain your freedom, do so. ²² For the one who was a slave when called to faith in the Lord is the Lord's freed person; similarly, the one who was free when called is Christ's slave. ²³ You were bought at a price; do not become slaves of human beings. ²⁴ Brothers and sisters, each person, as responsible to God, should remain in the situation they were in when God called them.

When we recognize the call of Christ and begin to respond to the good news in our hearts, we experience euphoria. In an excited moment, in a state of emotional instability, we might decide to change all aspects of our lives. We are mesmerized and overcome by the new vision we have been given.

At conversion, life takes on sudden and dramatic new meaning. Our old jobs, relationships, and friends become less relevant, at least momentarily, as we're carried away by the optimism. We're elevated in the buoyancy of the moment. Into these emotions, Paul writes today's passage, giving the Corinthians solid but staid advice.

Paul's advice was different than the calling of Christ to His disciples and different from Christ's response to the rich young ruler in Luke 18:18–30. To these specific individuals, the call was a command to follow Him and leave behind prior occupations.

The commands in 1 Corinthians seem to be an exception. Paul's advice for the newly converted Corinthians was for them to persist in their circumstances.

This in no way reflects an absence of spiritual change, which Paul emphasizes in his reflection on freedom (1 Corinthians 7:21–23). He writes of slaves becoming the Lord's freed people (1 Corinthians 7:22). He says that a slave who becomes a Christian can experience freedom from prior sin and condemnation in their new Christian existence.

Of course, this is also true for those who weren't slaves. All who come to believe in Jesus will have a sense of leaving their old lives behind. The unshackling we all experience isn't so much physical as spiritual and emotional.

Paul uses the word *apeleutheros* to describe being a freed person. This is a composite from *apo*, meaning "from," and *eleutheros*, meaning "free."

He reassures slaves that Christ, through His death and resurrection, bought their spiritual freedom. For one who had little, this was a wealthy gift. For one whose life had no future, it was a priceless promise. They were now Christ's. He would be responsible for their souls and justification. They were His freed people.

For those who were free before conversion, we might say they had liberty or fully expressed individualism. Paul wrote that they also had a responsibility. They were now partnered with Christ. They were now His, no longer free to behave as they wished; they were slaves, or adherents, to a new life.

Spiritually, both slave and libertarian were Christ's freed people.

This ideology is part of the shift in outlook Paul was at pains to explain. The Corinthian believers were no longer Corinthians; they were first and foremost Christians. Their spiritual magnetic field had shifted polarity from secularism to Christianity. In this shift, they were freed from their old ways but were now expected to follow a new direction as Christ's freed people. They were slaves to their new polarity in Christ.

On reflection, some might argue that neither the slave nor the libertarian was genuinely free, since they were both under Christ's lordship. Do we just substitute our bondage to earthly circumstances for bondage to Christ?

The truth is that conversion might outwardly appear to be a substitution of one form of slavery for another, but our ties to

Christ aren't formed under duress, nor are they maintained by bribery or fear of retribution.

Conversion cannot be considered slavery under any form of coercion. Our allegiance to Christ is forged through an open-handed choice and maintained by a desire to be in relationship with Him in recognition of His amazing grace. Swapped are the shackles of slavery for the bonds of a marriage-like relationship. We love, honour, and obey, for He first did likewise to win our freedom.

APPLICATION: FREED PERSON

- Reflect for a moment on your spiritual freedom. We are not condemned by our past or future. We are accepted and upheld in freedom by Jesus. We are empowered to behave as we wish, yet He is our choice. Thank Jesus for the freedom He has purchased for you.
- Pray for continued sensitivity not to overindulge your freedom but to be true to your new polarity in Christ.
- It may not always be possible to maintain the circumstances that existed at your conversion. Pray for the wisdom to know when change is necessary.

Undistracted Devotion

Now about virgins: I have no command from the Lord, but I give a judgment as one who by the Lord's mercy is trustworthy. [26] Because of the present crisis, I think that it is good for a man to remain as he is. [27] Are you pledged to a woman? Do not seek to be released. Are you free from such a commitment? Do not look for a wife. [28] But if you do marry, you have not sinned; and if a virgin marries, she has not sinned. But those who marry will face many troubles in this life, and I want to spare you this.

[29] What I mean, brothers and sisters, is that the time is short. From now on those who have wives should live as if they do not; [30] those who mourn, as if they did not; those who are happy, as if they were not; those who buy something, as if it were not theirs to keep; [31] those who use the things of the world, as if not engrossed in them. For this world in its present form is passing away.

[32] I would like you to be free from concern. An unmarried man is concerned about the Lord's affairs—how he can please the Lord. [33] But a married man is concerned about the affairs of this world—how he

can please his wife—[34] and his interests are divided. An unmarried woman or virgin is concerned about the Lord's affairs: Her aim is to be devoted to the Lord in both body and spirit. But a married woman is concerned about the affairs of this world—how she can please her husband. [35] I am saying this for your own good, not to restrict you, but that you may live in a right way in undivided devotion to the Lord.

[36] If anyone is worried that he might not be acting honorably toward the virgin he is engaged to, and if his passions are too strong and he feels he ought to marry, he should do as he wants. He is not sinning. They should get married. [37] But the man who has settled the matter in his own mind, who is under no compulsion but has control over his own will, and who has made up his mind not to marry the virgin—this man also does the right thing. [38] So then, he who marries the virgin does right, but he who does not marry her does better.

[39] A woman is bound to her husband as long as he lives. But if her husband dies, she is free to marry anyone she wishes, but he must belong to the Lord. [40] In my judgment, she is happier if she stays as she is—and I think that I too have the Spirit of God.

We can easily miss the point of Paul's writing if our focus is too narrow. Today's passage is a good example of when we might mistakenly concentrate on the specifics of relationships and miss the broader picture of how becoming a Christian changes our perspective on temporal matters.

Paul was responding to some specific questions from the Corinthians and his reply included direct answers and fresh perspectives to help them, and us, approach similar scenarios.

We would do well to note that Paul prefaces his specific comments with the reminder that he wasn't aware of any laws or direct teachings of Jesus on these matters.

In 1 Corinthians 7:29, Paul writes that he sees life on earth as a short-term situation that's at risk of ending abruptly. After all, Christ had promised to return.

Paul also addressed this dilemma, of whether to invest in earthly matters or simply give up, in 2 Thessalonians, where he had practical advice:

> We hear that some among you are idle and disruptive. They are not busy; they are busybodies. Such people we command and urge in the Lord Jesus Christ to settle down and earn the food they eat. And as for you, brothers and sisters, never tire of doing what is good. (2 Thessalonians 3:11–13)

Paul hoped to inspire the Thessalonians to never tire of doing good. He hoped to similarly inspire the Corinthians.

He had advice for all types of people, whether married, unmarried, betrothed, widowed, or single. He also offered advice regarding suitable partners and under what contexts separation and divorce might be acceptable. He states his aim in 1 Corinthians 7:35: *"I am saying this for your own good, not to restrict you, but that you may live in a right way in undivided devotion to the Lord."*

The idea of undivided devotion is linked to 1 Corinthians 7:32, where the Greek word for anxiety is derived from the word for divided. In both 1 Corinthians 7:32 and 7:35, Paul states his aim was: for his readers not to be divided or split between home, church, or family versus God. He wishes for them to be undistracted in their devotion to the Lord through having settled personal lives. In this way, they are best able to never tire of doing good.

The term "undivided devotion" is translated from the Greek *aperispastos euparedros*. *Aperispastos* conveys a subtle but similar meaning to the usual Greek word for undivided; it implies being drawn in different directions at the same time rather than being split. From this, some translations use the phrase "undistracted devotion." The Greek word translated as devotion is *euparedros*—which could be understood to refer to sitting in an attentive manner.

Paul, and presumably the Corinthians, understood that relationships tend to pull us in different directions and thus away from the Lord. Such misdirection inevitably makes us unable to sit in peace at His feet.

His goal for the married, single, betrothed, and widowed is for them to be able to sit peaceably at the feet of Christ. For those in a relationship with others, this means sitting together in stillness, in quiet devotion to Christ and His teaching.

Herein lies the challenge for couples. Can they still be a couple, close and intimate, yet also have undistracted attention on godly matters?

For those who are single, the challenge is to remain undistracted by thoughts of the opposite sex. Paul suggests this might be hard, and perhaps it's not something to struggle against lest we be further distracted.

More generally, this passage isn't just about relationships that lead us to distraction. Many temporal diversions tempt us away from Jesus and godly matters. Paul gives us the image of an attentive listener who isn't pulled in multiple directions, which naturally reminds us of Martha's sister Mary from Luke's gospel:

> "Martha, Martha," the Lord answered, "you are worried and upset about many things, but few things are needed—or indeed only one. Mary has chosen what is better, and it will not be taken away from her." (Luke 10:41–42)

It takes faith to lay down our diversions and focus on godly things. If we can achieve undistracted devotion, we can let go of our anxious thoughts and come before Him to rest. This is restorative and works for singles and couples alike.

APPLICATION: UNDISTRACTED DEVOTION

- Consider ways in which your quiet times can distract you. What can you do to make them less distracting?

- Take a few moments to quiet your thoughts before beginning your devotional time tomorrow so you might be able to sit peaceably and with attention.
- Pray that you would be less of a distraction to others as they seek to find undivided devotion before the Lord.

Stumbling Block

Now about food sacrificed to idols: We know that "We all possess knowledge." But knowledge puffs up while love builds up. [2] Those who think they know something do not yet know as they ought to know. [3] But whoever loves God is known by God.

[4] So then, about eating food sacrificed to idols: We know that "An idol is nothing at all in the world" and that "There is no God but one." [5] For even if there are so-called gods, whether in heaven or on earth (as indeed there are many "gods" and many "lords"), [6] yet for us there is but one God, the Father, from whom all things came and for whom we live; and there is but one Lord, Jesus Christ, through whom all things came and through whom we live.

[7] But not everyone possesses this knowledge. Some people are still so accustomed to idols that when they eat sacrificial food they think of it as having been sacrificed to a god, and since their conscience is weak, it is defiled. [8] But food does not bring us near to God; we are no worse if we do not eat, and no better if we do.

⁹ Be careful, however, that the exercise of your rights does not become a stumbling block to the weak. ¹⁰ For if someone with a weak conscience sees you, with all your knowledge, eating in an idol's temple, won't that person be emboldened to eat what is sacrificed to idols? ¹¹ So this weak brother or sister, for whom Christ died, is destroyed by your knowledge. ¹² When you sin against them in this way and wound their weak conscience, you sin against Christ. ¹³ Therefore, if what I eat causes my brother or sister to fall into sin, I will never eat meat again, so that I will not cause them to fall.

In 1 Corinthians 8, Paul offers some thoughts regarding the practice of sacrificing meat to idols, which is unlikely to be a pressing concern for most Christians. Even the tenuous link to halal meat is hardly relevant since its consumption can be readily avoided. In most Western countries, we have a choice of meats to purchase.

Other foibles come to mind that might be more relevant to modern Christians, such as celebrating Halloween or the use of alcohol, cannabis, and tobacco. In fact, it's not too difficult to think of controversies and become embroiled in them. It's important to find consensus on each of these hot potato issues, just as it was for the Corinthians to settle the issue of food preparation.

We might find Paul's advice to the Corinthians useful in managing our modern equivalents.

In 1 Corinthians 8:4–6, he dismisses idols. The implication is that since idols are worthless, their perceived evil is baseless. Although we might agree with Paul's reasoning, he does qualify this in 1 Corinthians 10:19–22:

> Do I mean then that food sacrificed to an idol is anything, or that an idol is anything? No, but the sacrifices of pagans are offered to demons, not to God, and I do not want you to be participants with demons. You cannot drink the cup of the Lord and the cup of demons too; you cannot have a part in both the Lord's table and the table of demons. Are we trying to arouse the Lord's jealousy? Are we stronger than he?

A caveat then might be that idols can be manmade but evil spiritual beings do exist and participating in their worship, intentionally or otherwise, tests God's ire. In light of this, perhaps prayerful circumspection would be wise in all controversial circumstances.

Paul goes on to highlight that these controversies are never our saving grace or means of sanctification, which belong to Christ alone.

Finally, in 1 Corinthians 8:9, Paul writes that our perspectives should not be a stumbling block for others. The Greek word for stumbling block is *proskomma*, a composite word from *pros* ("against") and *kopto* ("to strike"). The picture is that of catching our foot on a protruding object that causes us to trip. Whatever conclusions we come to on controversial topics, we should be mindful not to trip our brothers or sisters in Christ.

Paul's advice has echoes of Mark 9:42:

> If anyone causes one of these little ones—those who believe in me—to stumble, it would be better for them if a large millstone were hung around their neck and they were thrown into the sea.

In later chapters, he'll write that there are issues where absolutes do apply—for example, in 1 Corinthians 10:14–22. In many instances, though, it's possible to find a consensus that avoids leading people to stumble while providing sufficient liberty for others to enjoy God's gifts. Only in knowing Him can we find true wisdom in these issues.

APPLICATION: STUMBLING BLOCK

- Stumbling blocks are often issues that have no biblical precedents despite being important in society. Fashionable diets and alcohol abstinence come to mind, but there are others. Consider whether you may make unconscious choices that serve as stumbling blocks to others.
- In some matters, compromise is possible. Pray for wisdom to know what is fundamental versus what is negotiable.

- Understanding the choices of those we seek to evangelize can help us overcome our own inflexibility. Pray for compassion to ask sensitively and sincerely about people's life choices.

What is safe for one person may be quite unsafe for another. It has been said, and it is blessedly true, that God has his own secret stairway into every heart; but it is equally true that the devil has his own secret and subtle stairway into every heart. We may be strong enough to resist some temptation, but it may well be that someone else is not. Something may be no temptation whatever to us, but it may be a violent temptation to someone else. Therefore, in considering whether we will or will not do anything, we must think not only of its effect on us, but of its effect on others as well.[7]

—William Barclay

---

[7] Ibid., 89.

Hindrance

Am I not free? Am I not an apostle? Have I not seen Jesus our Lord? Are you not the result of my work in the Lord? [2] Even though I may not be an apostle to others, surely I am to you! For you are the seal of my apostleship in the Lord.

[3] This is my defense to those who sit in judgment on me. [4] Don't we have the right to food and drink? [5] Don't we have the right to take a believing wife along with us, as do the other apostles and the Lord's brothers and Cephas? [6] Or is it only I and Barnabas who lack the right to not work for a living?

[7] Who serves as a soldier at his own expense? Who plants a vineyard and does not eat its grapes? Who tends a flock and does not drink the milk? [8] Do I say this merely on human authority? Doesn't the Law say the same thing? [9] For it is written in the Law of Moses: "Do not muzzle an ox while it is treading out the grain." Is it about oxen that God is concerned? [10] Surely he says this for us, doesn't he? Yes, this was written for us, because whoever plows and threshes should be able to do so in the hope of sharing in the harvest. [11] If we have

sown spiritual seed among you, is it too much if we reap a material harvest from you? [12] If others have this right of support from you, shouldn't we have it all the more?

But we did not use this right. On the contrary, we put up with anything rather than hinder the gospel of Christ.

[13] Don't you know that those who serve in the temple get their food from the temple, and that those who serve at the altar share in what is offered on the altar? [14] In the same way, the Lord has commanded that those who preach the gospel should receive their living from the gospel.

[15] But I have not used any of these rights. And I am not writing this in the hope that you will do such things for me, for I would rather die than allow anyone to deprive me of this boast. [16] For when I preach the gospel, I cannot boast, since I am compelled to preach. Woe to me if I do not preach the gospel! [17] If I preach voluntarily, I have a reward; if not voluntarily, I am simply discharging the trust committed to me. [18] What then is my reward? Just this: that in preaching the gospel I may offer it free of charge, and so not make full use of my rights as a preacher of the gospel.

Here, Paul writes about whether payment is expected or discretionary for Christian ministry. In not requesting financial support from the Corinthians, in some people's eyes he had diminished his credibility as an apostle. In his practical style, Paul refutes this, declaring himself free to decline financial support and explaining that the Corinthians themselves are the justification of his apostleship.

Paul was in a unique position, as were the Corinthians. Both were navigating new circumstances in their lives. When Paul went to Corinth, he taught onto a blank canvas. There were plenty of other religions and beliefs in the city, but no one had preached Christianity. At this stage in history, the New Testament was being written in real-time. There had been no prior missionaries or outreach programs. No one had prepared the soil, or spoiled it. Paul had an opportunity to preach Christianity to an audience free of preconceptions or cynicism. He could challenge old behaviours and establish new practices that might become traditions. He could create an environment in which Christianity might flourish.

From this perspective, Paul's circumstances were radically different from ours in the twenty-first century. Our era has been characterized by a post-Christian ethic. Even the unchurched have some experience of Christianity, usually through ceremonial church services at landmark events or via the media. In the West, our pervasive lethargy or cynicism toward the church hinders people's natural curiosity about Jesus. Those we seek to reach already have half-constructed ideas concerning Christianity, one of which is the notion that the church is only interested in receiving our money for its own ends.

Paul's model of part-time tentmaker, part-time evangelist is rare today. In most mainstream denominations, the church funds pastors and church staff. The majority of staff aren't expected to find other employment.

In new or small churches with insufficient funds, a part-time pastor might need to supplement their income with secular earnings. Paul doesn't discourage this model. He seems to accept it. Although a pastor has the right to expect to be funded, he argues that deferring that right shouldn't be perceived as a slight on their credibility. *"On the contrary, we put up with anything rather than hinder the gospel of Christ,"* he writes in 1 Corinthians 9:12.

We know from reading of the challenges of Paul's life that this isn't an empty statement made for bravado. He sincerely lived to communicate Jesus's message and nothing would impair his ability to do this, whether financial or cultural.

The word hinder is translated from the Greek *egkope*, a composite word from *en* ("in") and *kopto* ("to cut down"). We might picture a tree being felled and laid across a trail. Such a hindrance is similar to a stumbling block, only larger.

Paul's goal was to remove potential barriers rather than create new ones. If declining financial assistance would accelerate the spread of the gospel, he would support that, even if it meant that he needed to work as a tentmaker.

We aren't usually faced with Paul's dilemma of whether to be paid for our Christian ministry. We are more often faced with other hindrances, including matters that aren't clearly defined in scripture.

The Corinthians' criticism was directed toward their minister, so we might reflect on whether we perceive hindrances, or personal annoyances, in those who minister to us. Just as finances represent a personal and private topic, some of these hindrances could be quite personal and require sensitive handling.

On a more corporate note, churches probably don't spend enough time considering whether they've set up unintentional roadblocks by trying to fit in with secular culture. If hindrances to the gospel do exist in modern churches, it follows that a church's public appearance should be a regular agenda item for any committee meeting.

Author Carl Trueman, in his book *Strange New World*, discusses countercultural ways in which the church can resist the unorthodox developments we have seen in the last twenty years. He suggests that our current culture places too much emphasis on feelings, especially introspection. This has led secular society on a merry dance to deny previous assumptions about selfhood. He suggests that churches should avoid worship styles or preaching that could perpetuate self-reflection and instead search for higher ground to see the beauty in reflecting on God, not the self.[8]

My sense is that Paul would agree with Trueman at least in principle. Yes, we should be willing to compromise, but we shouldn't create a mirage. We have been called to communicate a divine message. Anything less could be a hindrance to the gospel.

APPLICATION: HINDRANCE

- The idea of a tree being felled to block a highway reminds me of Matthew 7:3–5, where Jesus talks about a speck of dust and a plank. Pray that God would help you to identify any planks or felled trees

---

[8] Carl R. Trueman, *Strange New World* (Wheaton, IL: Crossway, 2022), 169–187.

in your ministry and help move them aside so as to remove obstacles to the gospel.

- Pray that your church would be a holy place, a place of reverence where the gospel is heard clearly and without hindrances.
- Pray for your ministerial staff. Their work isn't easy and their road is long. Consider ways in which you might support them or help remove hindrances to their evangelism.

Think about it: the Psalms present a view of the Christian life that is marked by joy but that also knows sorrow and loss. They set the struggles of the present in the context of God's great actions in times past and promises for the future. They help us to understand our status as strangers in a strange land. By setting forth a grand picture of God and the promise of future rest, they help us to keep perspective- theological and emotional- on the events of the present, whether personal, such as illness, or social, such as the disturbing transformations outlined in this book. We are creatures of emotions and sentiments, and we are fallen. Therefore, we need songs of redemption to help restore them to their proper context.[9]

—Carl R. Trueman

---

[9] Ibid., 182.

Christ's Law

Though I am free and belong to no one, I have made myself a slave to everyone, to win as many as possible. [20] To the Jews I became like a Jew, to win the Jews. To those under the law I became like one under the law (though I myself am not under the law), so as to win those under the law. [21] To those not having the law I became like one not having the law (though I am not free from God's law but am under Christ's law), so as to win those not having the law. [22] To the weak I became weak, to win the weak. I have become all things to all people so that by all possible means I might save some. [23] I do all this for the sake of the gospel, that I may share in its blessings.

[24] Do you not know that in a race all the runners run, but only one gets the prize? Run in such a way as to get the prize. [25] Everyone who competes in the games goes into strict training. They do it to get a crown that will not last, but we do it to get a crown that will last forever. [26] Therefore I do not run like someone running

aimlessly; I do not fight like a boxer beating the air. [27] No, I strike a blow to my body and make it my slave so that after I have preached to others, I myself will not be disqualified for the prize.

In these closing verses of 1 Corinthians 9, Paul summarizes his approach to the stumbling blocks and hindrances that beset the Corinthians. He offers two sporting analogies, which would have been familiar to the Corinthians, for Corinth hosted the Isthmian games, athletic competitions that were secondary in size and popularity only to those held in Olympia.

A phrase in the middle of our reading warrants further explanation, for it might easily be missed:

> To those not having the law I became like one not having the law (though I am not free from God's law but am under Christ's law), so as to win those not having the law. (1 Corinthians 9:21)

Paul isn't suggesting that we sin intentionally to reach those outside the church. According to author Ben Witherington III,

> He does not say that he became an idolator to idolators or an adulterer to adulterers. But in matters that he did not see as ethically or theologically essential or implied by the gospel, Paul believed in flexibility. This shows that the phrase "all things to all people"

is a part of Paul's demagogic rhetoric and is not to be taken literally.[10]

Instead Paul argues for an intention approach whereby we might put aside some of our cultural preferences to become more familiar with the unchurched. We might test our comfort zones and challenge ourselves to be more welcoming or adaptable to those we seek to appeal to.

Paul proposes an approach we might not have considered. In being all things to all people, he wants to ensure that we remain under the law of Christ. The idea of being bound to Christ's law is conveyed by the phrase *ennomos Christou* (1 Corinthians 9:21). Exactly what those boundaries might be, or what that might look like in reality, deserves some attention. It seems to have been Paul's modus operandi.

This also appears in Galatians 6:2: *"Carry each other's burdens, and in this way you will fulfill the law of Christ."* The use of the term in Galatians fits with Paul's stated desire to be accommodating to others. It also fits with one of the lessons from Christ's ministry, that we are to love our neighbour as ourselves (Mark 12:31, Matthew 7:12, Luke 6:31).

But I wonder whether Christ's law (*ennomos Christou*) is about more than this. A central part of Jesus's ministry was the cross, and I am perpetually challenged by His provoking state-

---

[10] Ben Witherington III, *Conflict and Community in Corinth: A Sociorhetorical Commentary on 1 and 2 Corinthians* (Grand Rapids, MI: William B Eerdmans, 1995), 213.

ments regarding carrying our crosses (Matthew 10:38, Mark 8:34, Luke 9:23, 27).

We read in Luke 14:27, *"And whoever does not carry their cross and follow me cannot be my disciple."* This speaks to the heart of *ennomos Christou.* Carrying one another burdens is a manifestation of obeying the command to carry one's cross, which goes further than simply being neighbourly as a good Samaritan.

When we carry our crosses, we don't just carry our own burdens; we sacrifice them along with our own desires for the sake of doing His will. Yes, there is the labour and toil from carrying the cross itself, but there is also the pain of giving up on our own aspirations for the sake of His.

Proverbs 16:9 tells us, *"The heart of man plans his way, but the Lord establishes his steps"* (ESV).

My sense is that it's hard for us to work out what this looks like in our lives. Perhaps this is why we are called to do it daily. If it can become a routine, perhaps we might more intuitively know what this sacrificial giving of our time, preferences, and energy looks like.

In the sense of sacrificial giving, Christ's law speaks to the *agape* love of 1 John 3:16 and the love Paul will shortly define in 1 Corinthians 13.

We have gone from acts of service and carrying burdens to mental alignments and disciplining ourselves to carry our crosses. And finally we come to the heart of the matter: Paul acts as he does, to those he seeks to reach, because he loves them.

APPLICATION: CHRIST'S LAW

- Consider what you think Paul meant by writing about *ennomos Christou*. What was different about Christ's ministry that established a different law than the Old Testament, or perhaps a new interpretation of it?
- Paul's attitude toward evangelism is challenging. He was incredibly dedicated. If we had even an ounce of his passion for the lost, I think we would achieve much more. Thank God for Paul's ministry and ask for Christ's law to be the benchmark for your own evangelism.
- If Christ's law has hands (acts), a head, (obedience), and a heart (love), pray that each of these would be the hallmarks of your own attitudes, just as they were for Paul.

Share

For I do not want you to be ignorant of the fact, brothers and sisters, that our ancestors were all under the cloud and that they all passed through the sea. ² They were all baptized into Moses in the cloud and in the sea. ³ They all ate the same spiritual food ⁴ and drank the same spiritual drink; for they drank from the spiritual rock that accompanied them, and that rock was Christ. ⁵ Nevertheless, God was not pleased with most of them; their bodies were scattered in the wilderness.

⁶ Now these things occurred as examples to keep us from setting our hearts on evil things as they did. ⁷ Do not be idolaters, as some of them were; as it is written: "The people sat down to eat and drink and got up to indulge in revelry." ⁸ We should not commit sexual immorality, as some of them did—and in one day twenty-three thousand of them died. ⁹ We should not test Christ, as some of them did—and were killed by snakes. ¹⁰ And do not grumble, as some of them did—and were killed by the destroying angel.

¹¹ These things happened to them as examples and were written down as warnings for us, on whom the

culmination of the ages has come. [12] So, if you think you are standing firm, be careful that you don't fall! [13] No temptation has overtaken you except what is common to mankind. And God is faithful; he will not let you be tempted beyond what you can bear. But when you are tempted, he will also provide a way out so that you can endure it.

[14] Therefore, my dear friends, flee from idolatry. [15] I speak to sensible people; judge for yourselves what I say. [16] Is not the cup of thanksgiving for which we give thanks a participation in the blood of Christ? And is not the bread that we break a participation in the body of Christ? [17] Because there is one loaf, we, who are many, are one body, for we all share the one loaf.

[18] Consider the people of Israel: Do not those who eat the sacrifices participate in the altar? [19] Do I mean then that food sacrificed to an idol is anything, or that an idol is anything? [20] No, but the sacrifices of pagans are offered to demons, not to God, and I do not want you to be participants with demons. [21] You cannot drink the cup of the Lord and the cup of demons too; you cannot have a part in both the Lord's table and the table of demons. [22] Are we trying to arouse the Lord's jealousy? Are we stronger than he?

Paul works to persuade strong, self-confident Corinthians not to continue with their old practices and instead be saved by Christ. He takes a patient approach, one which we can read through our Christian lens with diffidence since we aren't intimately connected with the issues at hand in this passage. We don't participate in idol sacrifices, nor do we join in other licentious behaviours that Corinth was infamous for.

If we read this passage only feigning interest, we lose the opportunity to see Paul at work—and we miss the potential to learn from his approach. We would do well to read carefully how Paul went about challenging the congregation to change their religious perspectives.

Trying to convince others of the error of their ways often leads to emotive arguments that leave each party more firmly entrenched in their original view. The gifted speaker is able to encourage his audience to emerge from their trench—not with a gun, but with a soccer ball, willing to play.

The goal of a good discussion is not to pin down your opponent with relentless attacks. It's about bringing them to a better understanding of your own position. Winning outright isn't everything; making progress in a debate can be more meaningful.

In these verses, Paul moves his readers in a masterly way. He uses the notion of sharing to appeal to the logic of distractors.

He begins in 1 Corinthians 10:1–4 by establishing the Jews' theological precedents as forefathers of the Christian faith. The Jews who left Egypt enjoyed God's saving favour as they travelled through the Red Sea. They saw God's spiritual blessing in a pillar of cloud and His practical blessing in receiving food and water in the desert. He emphasizes how privileged and full of godly favour the Jews were.

Despite their favour, however, their rebellious behaviour led to their destruction (1 Corinthians 10:6–11). The implications would have been clear to the strong, self-confident Corinthians: there is a precedent for unfavourable outcomes when you continually put God to the test.

Paul goes on to explain that the people aren't alone in their temptations. Not all give in. Many resist. God provides a literal escape route, a hidden path that enables believers to resist.

He goes on to remind them of their participation in the sharing of bread, which was symbolic of Christ's last supper (1 Corinthians 10:14–17). The shared loaf served as a metaphor for their belief that a man surrendered his life to demonstrate the might of God's power and grace.

The Greek word translated as participation in 1 Corinthians 10:16 is *koinonia*, which stems from *koinos*, meaning "common." It indicates a partnership, joint venture, combined activity, or community.

Thus, at the heart of Paul's appeal in 1 Corinthians 10:10 is the idea that we are members of a blessed family. He encourages those who would leave the family to come back and not be tempted by spiritual and physical dalliances outside the family of Christ.

In the modern church, our communion wafers are a pitiful token of the intimate meal shared between Jesus and His disciples. When Jesus's death was still a very raw memory, the impact of splitting a loaf between believers would have been much more evocative. This bread wasn't bought at the grocery store. It had to be made. The yeast, flour, and olive oil all had to be sourced. Effort went into producing it. Sharing the meal was a visual representation of the people's belief, their own conversions and willingness to associate with each other and God.

It has been suggested that the bread represents our fellowship with one another as the body of Christ, whereas the wine represents our spiritual fellowship with Jesus. By sharing in the cup, we share in the notion of spiritual sacrifice, burying ourselves as we become new creations in Christ. In that sense, we cannot drink from the cup of Christ and continue to make offerings to demons. The two are mutually exclusive.

Through this rhetoric of shared experiences, Paul delivers the Corinthians to his final candid comment. If he had started with this, it would have surely led his distractors to dismiss the rest of his argument.

He writes, *"Are we trying to arouse the Lord's jealousy? Are we stronger than he?"* (1 Corinthians 10:22) The answer, of course, is that we aren't stronger than God. But the fact that so much rhetoric was required to deliver us to this point of agreement indicates how strong the Corinthians thought they were.

There is a parallel here. At times, we subconsciously harbour similar perspectives today. In response, Paul would call us back to our shared experiences in the body of Christ, to shared worship, communal prayer, and enjoying the fellowship of the bread and the wine.

APPLICATION: SHARE

- Consider the experiences you share with other Christians. Thank God for their fellowship and shared witness.
- Next time you're in church, take a moment to reflect on the miracle of sharing in the blessing of the service with other Christians.
- Thank God for Paul's ability to appeal to people's reason. I'm sure Paul reflected any praise he received back to God and the Holy Spirit. Pray that the Holy Spirit would provide you with original approaches like Paul's when you face difficult conversations.

Seek

"I have the right to do anything," you say—but not everything is beneficial. "I have the right to do anything"—but not everything is constructive. ²⁴ No one should seek their own good, but the good of others.

²⁵ Eat anything sold in the meat market without raising questions of conscience, ²⁶ for, "The earth is the Lord's, and everything in it."

²⁷ If an unbeliever invites you to a meal and you want to go, eat whatever is put before you without raising questions of conscience. ²⁸ But if someone says to you, "This has been offered in sacrifice," then do not eat it, both for the sake of the one who told you and for the sake of conscience. ²⁹ I am referring to the other person's conscience, not yours. For why is my freedom being judged by another's conscience? ³⁰ If I take part in the meal with thankfulness, why am I denounced because of something I thank God for?

³¹ So whether you eat or drink or whatever you do, do it all for the glory of God. ³² Do not cause anyone to stumble, whether Jews, Greeks or the church of God—³³ even as I try to please everyone in every way. For I am

not seeking my own good but the good of many, so that they may be saved.

¹ Follow my example, as I follow the example of Christ.

Paul continues in his discussion of the issues plaguing the Corinthian church. They had started as fine print and risen to become headlines. In this passage, we encounter more advice about eating meat that has been sacrificed to idols, as well as some general comments about righteous attitudes.

At the start of our passage, Paul evokes contemporary arguments from the philosophers of Corinth, which we would today characterize as expressive individualism, which takes the position that man is free to express himself as he feels and that it's society that limits this freedom.[11]

Expressive individualism contends that man is most authentic when he is able to freely express what's in his heart. This philosophy is at odds with orthodox Christianity, which contends rather that a man is born in sin; left to his own urges and desires, his heart will lead him astray from godly wisdom.

Paul tackles the fallacy of expressive individualism by pointing to its personal and corporate failings; it's not always personally beneficial, nor is it consistently edifying for organizations. We see Paul's wisdom in the many stories around us of personal ruin and organizational decline when people pursue individual freedoms at the expense of others.

---

[11] Trueman, *Strange New World*, 22–23.

His remedy is that the Corinthians should not *"seek their own good, but the good of others"* (1 Corinthians 10:24). This is book-ended by what he writes in 1 Corinthians 11:1, *"Follow my example, as I follow the example of Christ."*

So we should seek the good of others and follow Christ. We are not to seek the good of the self and follow our vanity.

The Greek word for seek is *zeteo*, which coveys not an absentminded glance but rather an earnest attempt to find what we're looking for. With *zeteo*, we prioritize the search. Paul's message for the Corinthians is for them to intentionally seek the good of others.

When we conceive of our church disputes in this manner, it will clarify our positions and purify our motives. Once our discussions become other-centric, we are able to give over our disputes to God, for they are not ours alone. We can trust Him to find common ground, if that's possible, and trust His wisdom to build compromise.

For Paul, compromise was possible in the matter of eating different foods, although he did have absolutes (1 Corinthians 10:28). He drew an exception in instances when it became clear that disagreement would be more beneficial than compromise. He sometimes took the long view and declined hospitality.

Paul concludes that the Corinthians should follow his example and that of Jesus. Our goal as Christians, whenever possible, is to mirror Jesus, to follow Him, and in doing so serve as an example to those around us.

This is not an easy task, but we should pay attention to our behaviour, lest we become self-centred and legalistic. Our attention should be on Him whom we confess to follow. Only in following Him do we become an example to others. If we seek Jesus earnestly and with conviction, we will be better positioned to follow Him and not our own hearts.

We should hope to demonstrate expressive Christianity, not expressive individualism. Some in the Corinthian church seemed to have gotten this the wrong way round, perhaps because they weren't looking in the right direction or were looking with disinterest.

APPLICATION: SEEK

- The act of earnestly looking brings with it the expectation that we'll find what we're searching for. Pray for this attitude of heart when you spend time with Jesus and in His word.
- Paul's message was both personal and corporate. Pray that your own church would continue to search for Jesus with intent and purpose.
- If you are in dispute over matters of doctrinal differences, pray for the courage to hand the dispute over to God and give yourself the task of praying for the hearts of those who oppose you—not that their opinions would change, but that they would see Jesus in your actions.

We can do all things to the glory of God only when we remember the duty we must discharge to one another;

and we will do that only when we remember that our Christian freedom is given to us not for our own sake but for the sake of others.[12]

—William Barclay

---

[12] Barclay, *The New Daily Study Bible*, 122.

Image and Glory

I praise you for remembering me in everything and for holding to the traditions just as I passed them on to you. ³ But I want you to realize that the head of every man is Christ, and the head of the woman is man, and the head of Christ is God. ⁴ Every man who prays or prophesies with his head covered dishonors his head. ⁵ But every woman who prays or prophesies with her head uncovered dishonors her head—it is the same as having her head shaved. ⁶ For if a woman does not cover her head, she might as well have her hair cut off; but if it is a disgrace for a woman to have her hair cut off or her head shaved, then she should cover her head.

⁷ A man ought not to cover his head, since he is the image and glory of God; but woman is the glory of man. ⁸ For man did not come from woman, but woman from man; ⁹ neither was man created for woman, but woman for man. ¹⁰ It is for this reason that a woman ought to have authority over her own head, because of the angels. ¹¹ Nevertheless, in the Lord woman is not independent of man, nor is man independent of wom-

an. ¹² For as woman came from man, so also man is born of woman. But everything comes from God.

¹³ Judge for yourselves: Is it proper for a woman to pray to God with her head uncovered? ¹⁴ Does not the very nature of things teach you that if a man has long hair, it is a disgrace to him, ¹⁵ but that if a woman has long hair, it is her glory? For long hair is given to her as a covering. ¹⁶ If anyone wants to be contentious about this, we have no other practice—nor do the churches of God.

In the middle of today's verses, Paul links the image of man and the glory of God (1 Corinthians 11:7). We were made in God's image, and that image can bring glory to God.

The concept of being made in another's image is broad, but it includes appearance. This is relevant for the rest of today's passage. It can also include character, personality, behaviour, and conversation, encompassing all that makes us unique yet created to reflect the glory of God.

We bring glory to God through our lives. As such, He can be reflected in our actions and thoughtfulness. It has often been remarked that the church serves as the hands and feet of Jesus. For those hands and feet, it is an honour to bring glory to God and reflect, if only in a dim and burnished sense, the magnificence of His glory (Isaiah 43:6–7).

In our modern times, much is made of not being prejudicial against a person's appearance. There is truth to the goodness of this attitude. We are told in 1 Samuel that the Lord judges according to the heart (1 Samuel 16:7). But we are also told, in the same verse, that man judges by the outward appearance. We have an intrinsic reflex to assess others based on what we see and how they present themselves. This means that we will intrinsically notice if they present themselves in a manner that honours God. Our image, in its fullness, reflects the glory of God (1 Corinthians 11:7, 1 Samuel 16:7, Isaiah 43:6–7).

In today's passage, Paul addresses concerns about corporate appearances during public worship in the church.

The Corinthians had accepted Christ's lordship in their lives and were seeking to bring honour and glory to God through their ministrations during church services. Paul spent the previous few chapters urging them to remove stumbling blocks and traps that might confuse weaker or less mature Christians.

Unfortunately, some of his words in today's passage might undermine this prior work and cause confusion in modern readers. This would not have been his aim, of course, nor the Holy Spirit who inspired his writing.

I'm referring to the subordination of women/wives (1 Corinthians 11:3), headwear fashion in the church, and the purpose of women/wives to honour their men/husbands (1 Corinthians 11:7). These are contentious issues to us, just as they were to Corinthians, partly due to the fact that we share similar beliefs to the Corinthians prior to our conversion.

Hopefully we didn't believe in the plethora of Greek and Roman gods or attend the parties in Aphrodite's temple, but we *were* driven by self-fulfilment and the pursuit of those activities that brought us happiness. Like the Corinthians, we have pursued life, liberty, and freedom through self-expression and self-contentment. At the core of this philosophy is the selfish desire to glorify the self above others, and certainly above our creator God.

At conversion, we transition from this perspective to one which is Christ-centred. We reflect on the life of Christ and open our eyes, revealing a great mystery. Once we conceive that the centre of our lives is not ourselves but God, we abdicate the throne. We desire to bring glory to our creator, which is our purpose (Isaiah 43:6–7).

Most often, the life we are called to live is similar, from the outside, to our pre-conversion existence. We may do many of the same things, maintain the same profession, and enjoy the same leisure pursuits, but our hearts are changed. Following conversion, we are ready to be taught by God to demonstrate honour that is befitting to our Lord.

In this context, Paul's ideas are less inflammatory.

Also note that the Greek words for man and woman are the same as those for husband and wife, respectively. The way they're translated depends on the context in which they're used.

Here and elsewhere, Paul writes that there should be order in a marriage.

The husband has authority or headship, just as Christ has headship over His church. The image of Christ's headship is a challenging perspective for men to follow. Christ-like headship, appropriately understood, speaks of service, sacrifice, and selflessness. Christ had purpose; He didn't flit manically from meeting one need to another. His purpose, like ours, was to glorify God. A husband who seeks first to bring glory to God isn't an argumentative partner who exercises his authority without love.

To inspire women, Paul recounts the creation story. Women, like men, were created in the image of God and for His glory. In Genesis, Eve was also to bring fulfilment to her husband; without her, he was isolated and without companionship.

Paul goes on to highlight the fact that men and women are intrinsically linked before God. Neither has independence from the other. They are equal in their need for each other and God.

Paul expected women to be present in the Corinthian church services. He expected them to participate. This was a break from Jewish tradition, as well as from the patriarchal society of the first century.

He goes on to say that men and women should be distinguishable from each other while in church. Men should look like men and women like women. These would not have been inflammatory, since head coverings were common at that time. In the first century, a woman's head covering was an emblem of dignity, authority, and stature.

Although we might mock this today and think of it as suppressive, that was not Paul's objective.

Modern equivalents to the first-century head covering might be modest dress or makeup.

Paul also believed that a person's dress should not be a distraction in church (1 Corinthians 11:10). A rabbinic tradition, perhaps born of Genesis 6, held that angels could be led into temptation by a woman's beauty. The weakness of these celestial beings was seen as a reason to be mindful of church attire, in case one of their kind were present.

Whether we hold to this tradition or not, mortal men were present at church, men who were no doubt of weaker spiritual backbone than their celestial cousins and presumably might also be distracted by inappropriate female attire.

In 1 Corinthians 11:14–15, Paul writes of hair fashions in Corinth, stressing how appearances and the celebration of manhood and womanhood in the church are opportunities to bring glory to God.

This passage is far from irrelevant in the twenty-first century. Image and appearance are still important. When we're able, especially in public worship, we should seek to honour God with our appearance. The exact outworking of this will vary, but it wouldn't be appropriate for a man to worship God with bright red lipstick nor would it be fitting for a woman to preach while scantily dressed.

Both of these examples might be mistaken for the kind of lifestyles that were rife in first-century Corinth.

Paul's words are timely, since our secular world encourages self-expression as a means of conveying our authenticity. We need to be mindful that we reflect Him in how we express ourselves.

APPLICATION: IMAGE AND GLORY

- We might not care for Paul's comments here, yet there is truth in them. The way we present ourselves isn't limited to our clothes or hairstyles; it includes how we behave. As a Christian, our appearances should bring glory to God. What that looks like will be unique to the individual, but pray that He would show you whether any of your traits don't glorify Him.

- Paul doesn't suggest that these issues affect our salvation, nor would non-Christians be expected to adhere to them. He is encouraging unity among us as we abandon arguments over these matters, which will be important if we are to glorify God and not our own selfish ideas. Pray that your church's leadership team will find consensus so your congregation may continue to glorify God.

- At first reading, these verses might be offensive to some. Pray that the Holy Spirit would provide insight into the truth. The ideas may be contentious, but we can learn wisdom if our goal is to bring Him glory through our lives.

Biblical teachability comes out of burning desire to see God glorified by our lives and actions. Our passion for God's glory gives us strength to face the humiliation of accepting our faults. Our aim is not to show our abilities to the world. It is to show God's abilities. We gladly accept any help we can get to glorify God, even if we must endure being humbled.[13]

—Ajith Fernando

---

[13] Ajith Fernando, *Reclaiming Friendship* (Waterloo, ON: Herald Press, 1993), 113.

Remembrance

In the following directives I have no praise for you, for your meetings do more harm than good. [18] In the first place, I hear that when you come together as a church, there are divisions among you, and to some extent I believe it. [19] No doubt there have to be differences among you to show which of you have God's approval. 20 So then, when you come together, it is not the Lord's Supper you eat, [21] for when you are eating, some of you go ahead with your own private suppers. As a result, one person remains hungry and another gets drunk. [22] Don't you have homes to eat and drink in? Or do you despise the church of God by humiliating those who have nothing? What shall I say to you? Shall I praise you? Certainly not in this matter!

[23] For I received from the Lord what I also passed on to you: The Lord Jesus, on the night he was betrayed, took bread, [24] and when he had given thanks, he broke it and said, "This is my body, which is for you; do this in remembrance of me." [25] In the same way, after supper he took the cup, saying, "This cup is the new covenant in my blood; do this, whenever you drink it, in remembrance

of me." [26] For whenever you eat this bread and drink this cup, you proclaim the Lord's death until he comes.

[27] So then, whoever eats the bread or drinks the cup of the Lord in an unworthy manner will be guilty of sinning against the body and blood of the Lord. [28] Everyone ought to examine themselves before they eat of the bread and drink from the cup. [29] For those who eat and drink without discerning the body of Christ eat and drink judgment on themselves. [30] That is why many among you are weak and sick, and a number of you have fallen asleep. [31] But if we were more discerning with regard to ourselves, we would not come under such judgment. [32] Nevertheless, when we are judged in this way by the Lord, we are being disciplined so that we will not be finally condemned with the world.

[33] So then, my brothers and sisters, when you gather to eat, you should all eat together. [34] Anyone who is hungry should eat something at home, so that when you meet together it may not result in judgment.

And when I come I will give further directions.

In this passage, Paul addresses the attitudes of the Corinthians as they remembered the gift of Christ given through His sacrifice. Paul was concerned that the church's attitudes didn't befit the transcendental nature of Christ's gift.

Memories are important to us. They refresh our motives and intentions, recentring us and guiding our actions. They help us recognize the recurrence of patterns in our lives. Memories can also be made through all our senses—sight, hearing, touch, smell, and taste. To these, I would add that we can also make memories through our emotions.

How the church remembers the cross is critical. If the gift of the cross is portrayed as a frivolous gesture, this diminishes the gift's ability to alter people's lives, change their behaviours, and convince others of its worth.

Paul has been at pains to make sure that the image of the church in Corinth wasn't tainted by the behaviour of errant Christians. He instructs about how Christ's sacrifice is to be remembered.

It's worth noting, as author William Barclay does, that this account of the celebration of communion was one of the first to be recorded in the New Testament.[14] First Corinthians was written around AD 55, before the gospel accounts. Paul uses the descriptions he was given by the apostles to recount the events of the last supper as Jesus shared bread and wine. It's a familiar scene to us today.

Although Christian denominations may vary in their interpretations of the meaning of these elements, it is agreed that sharing bread and wine is an act of remembrance. The Greek word for remembrance is *anamnesis*, from *ana* ("again") and *mimnesko* ("to remember"). We are to remember again what Jesus accomplished through His crucifixion and resurrection.

It appears that some in the Corinthian church had slipped into a less formal pattern of remembrance and had begun to celebrate in a way that caused divisions and led some astray. Paul reminded them of the solemnity of the occasion.

[14] Barclay, *The New Daily Study Bible*, 121.

I suspect that none of the Corinthians had been present at Golgotha. I also suspect they didn't like to be reminded of the cruel details of Jesus's torture and death. We hold this in common with the Corinthians.

The purpose of remembrance is to move us to appreciation. Partaking of the bread and wine serves to create a symbolic moment in which to connect our hearts and minds with our beliefs.

If the heart is the seat of our emotions, then stirring up the emotion of Christ's suffering will empower us. If the mind is the seat of our consciousness, the memory of Christ will trigger us. Connecting them through this act of remembrance brings us unity and purpose. We are moved to follow Him more closely and with greater certainty. Through communion, we are moved by our appreciation of the memory to love His ways.

Paul desires for the Corinthians to rethink their attitudes toward the act of the Lord's supper—and through his writing, we have a similar opportunity.

He marvels at the power and wisdom of the cross. At the Lord's supper, we are brought painfully to the foot of the cross as we seek to remember those events. Paul would have us stay there and remember that Christ rose. The New Covenant wasn't solely forged on the cross, but it was completed through His resurrection, ascension, and the gift of the Holy Spirit.

There is joy in mourning at the Lord's supper, which can be appreciated through this pattern of solemn remembrance followed by sober celebration of His resurrection and our call to a new life.

APPLICATION: REMEMBRANCE

- Our attitudes to the Lord's supper are both personal and corporate. They will be influenced by your denomination's approach. Please pray that these occasions would give you an opportunity to pause and reflect, refocusing on Christ.
- Pray that the attitudes in your church would mirror the standards that Paul set for the Corinthians so the celebration of the Lord's supper would be a fitting tribute to His amazing gift.
- How non-Christians see the purpose of the Lord's supper reflects how it is performed and understood by Christians. Pray earnestly for Jesus to teach you what He meant at the last supper when He inaugurated this tradition (Mark 14:22–25, Luke 22:18–20).

Common Good

Now about the gifts of the Spirit, brothers and sisters, I do not want you to be uninformed. ² You know that when you were pagans, somehow or other you were influenced and led astray to mute idols. ³ Therefore I want you to know that no one who is speaking by the Spirit of God says, "Jesus be cursed," and no one can say, "Jesus is Lord," except by the Holy Spirit.

⁴ There are different kinds of gifts, but the same Spirit distributes them. ⁵ There are different kinds of service, but the same Lord. ⁶ There are different kinds of working, but in all of them and in everyone it is the same God at work.

⁷ Now to each one the manifestation of the Spirit is given for the common good. ⁸ To one there is given through the Spirit a message of wisdom, to another a message of knowledge by means of the same Spirit, ⁹ to another faith by the same Spirit, to another gifts of healing by that one Spirit, ¹⁰ to another miraculous powers, to another prophecy, to another distinguishing between spirits, to another speaking in different kinds of tongues, and to still another the interpretation of

tongues. [11] All these are the work of one and the same Spirit, and he distributes them to each one, just as he determines.

O n a scale with apologetics at one end and spirituality at the other, I would be closer to the apologetics end. And I suspect I would have more in common with Christian writers Lee Strobel (*The Case for Christ*), Josh McDowell (*Evidence that Demands a Verdict*), and Frank Morison (*Who Moved the Stone*) than Ajith Fernando, Corrie Ten Boom, or Dietrich Bonhoeffer. In my defence, I would not have been out of place amongst the disciples who seemed to be bereft of spiritual insight. Perhaps I would have found a close friend in Paul, who as Saul failed to recognize Jesus for who he was during His three years of earthly ministry.

For Saul and most of the disciples, it took an act of spirituality for them to break away from an apologetics perspective and embrace a more spiritual outlook. For the disciples, it was the resurrection and upper room experience. For Saul, it was the road to Damascus.

In his new life as Paul, the former Saul understood that there was a mystery to the gospel that required a revelation or insight to perceive the truth about Christ (Colossians 4:3, Ephesians 3:8–9). This wasn't special knowledge gained through learning but perception given by spiritual insight. Thus, even for apologists like Paul, a spiritual dimension underpinned their belief in Jesus—and Paul speaks to this in today's passage.

Spirituality also puzzled C.S. Lewis, who was familiar with emotional responses to literature and the arts but recognized that spirituality was something more.

> If I find in myself a desire which no experience in this world can satisfy, the most probable explanation is that I was made for another world. If none of my earthy pleasures satisfy it, that does not prove that the universe is a fraud. Probably earthly pleasures were never meant to satisfy it, but only to arouse it, to suggest the real thing.[15]

Spirituality is more than the warm, comfortable glow a person feels from an excellent worship song. Although there is much good to be said in aiming for warm feelings, I can't help but think the concept Paul writes about here, and experienced by the earlier Christians, is about something greater.

Paul was concerned that the Corinthians were being symbolic in their expression of the Holy Spirit. He encourages them to continue to express their spirituality but to do so in a manner that uplifts the whole church.

The word Paul uses for manifestation is *phanerosis*, which can be translated in terms of making something apparent or bringing it to light. It's a disclosure. This is similar to *Pharos*, the Greek word for a lighthouse. Just as a lighthouse brings light to hidden rocks, so *phanerosis* breaks through the spiritual darkness to shine a light on God.

---

[15] C.S. Lewis, *Mere Christianity* (New York, NY: MacMillian, 1960), 120.

Sometimes those who are spiritual might not perceive their spirituality, just like a lighthouse keeper. Those looking on can see that light and benefit from it.

Perhaps the analogy of the lighthouse also speaks to the idea that we should be on the lookout for spiritual things. If we miss the lighthouse, we may miss the opportunity to be encouraged and reach home safely.

Paul describes the expression of the Holy Spirit as being for the common good (1 Corinthians 12:7). The Greek word for common good is *sumphero*, a composite of *sum* ("together") and *phero* ("bring"). Acts of spirituality should have the effect of bringing a church together in unity.

Paul is continuing his instructions for corporate worship. In that setting, public displays of spirituality shouldn't be divisive. If these spiritual acts are genuine, there should be something other-worldly, miraculous, and community-oriented about them.

Public expressions of spirituality are emotionally perplexing. Jesus made spiritual displays in public and they were often mis-understood and unappreciated as a sign of His spirituality for the first-century witnesses.

Whatever public spiritual displays we make, we are unlikely to make examples as grand as those of Christ—feeding the five thousand, raising Lazarus—nor should we seek opportunities for such displays; that would be self-aggrandizement. With grace, we need to be open to the possibility that some in our churches may be spiritually gifted in the ways Paul discusses.

Jesus also made private displays of spirituality—his interac-tion with the woman at the well, healing Peter's mother, healing the centurion's daughter, and healing the woman who touched his cloak. Those who experienced His private ministry seemed to better perceive the nature of His spirituality. Those who were healed or given prophecy knew they had experienced God.

Although I wouldn't want to suppress corporate expressions of spirituality, perhaps there is something significant in this observation. Our personal experiences of God have a more telling effect on our beliefs than the dramatic spiritual encounters for which we sometimes yearn. Maybe that's why personal devotions are so important in our spiritual lives.

When our personal spiritual experiences can lift others and point to Christ, Paul says it would be fitting to share them. The goal of sharing is for others to receive light from His lighthouse and be brought closer to Him for the common good.

APPLICATION: COMMON GOOD

- Take a few moments to consider your approach to spiritual matters. How comfortable do you feel about words of wisdom or knowledge? How about when you hear someone speak in tongues?
- Pray that God would give you the grace to accept that spiritual manifestations are to be expected in the enlightened. May He enable you to discern when such acts are genuine.
- Symbolism has a role in corporate worship. But for spiritual matters, corporately at least, spontaneity is often the norm. It isn't easy to get comfortable with

the unexpected. Pray that your church would find a common ground between apologetics and spirituality. Let's not be too blind to the opportunity that we miss the light on the horizon.

I suspect that just as "charismania", an overemphasis on prophecy or tongues, is not healthy, neither is "charisphobia", the anathematizing of all such gifts. We are not called to act in the chaotic and selfish fashion the Corinthians did, but we are also not called on to quench the Spirit and arrange Christian worship so that there is no room for the spontaneous Word from above to be shared. There is a balance between Spirit and structure, order and spontaneity that should be maintained in any local congregation.[16]

—Ben Witherington III

---

[16] Witherington, *Conflict and Community in Corinth*, 263.

Body

Just as a body, though one, has many parts, but all its many parts form one body, so it is with Christ. [13] For we were all baptized by one Spirit so as to form one body—whether Jews or Gentiles, slave or free—and we were all given the one Spirit to drink. [14] Even so the body is not made up of one part but of many.

[15] Now if the foot should say, "Because I am not a hand, I do not belong to the body," it would not for that reason stop being part of the body. [16] And if the ear should say, "Because I am not an eye, I do not belong to the body," it would not for that reason stop being part of the body. [17] If the whole body were an eye, where would the sense of hearing be? If the whole body were an ear, where would the sense of smell be? [18] But in fact God has placed the parts in the body, every one of them, just as he wanted them to be. [19] If they were all one part, where would the body be? [20] As it is, there are many parts, but one body.

[21] The eye cannot say to the hand, "I don't need you!" And the head cannot say to the feet, "I don't need you!" [22] On the contrary, those parts of the body that

seem to be weaker are indispensable, [23] and the parts that we think are less honorable we treat with special honor. And the parts that are unpresentable are treated with special modesty, [24] while our presentable parts need no special treatment. But God has put the body together, giving greater honor to the parts that lacked it, [25] so that there should be no division in the body, but that its parts should have equal concern for each other. [26] If one part suffers, every part suffers with it; if one part is honored, every part rejoices with it.

[27] Now you are the body of Christ, and each one of you is a part of it. [28] And God has placed in the church first of all apostles, second prophets, third teachers, then miracles, then gifts of healing, of helping, of guidance, and of different kinds of tongues. [29] Are all apostles? Are all prophets? Are all teachers? Do all work miracles? [30] Do all have gifts of healing? Do all speak in tongues? Do all interpret? [31] Now eagerly desire the greater gifts.

I recently came across the term "body theology" in a short book by Ajith Fernando titled *Reclaiming Friendship*. He writes,

When a group shows concern and sensitivity to visions and gifts of its workers, it affirms a crucial aspect of what we may call "body theology". According to this theology, the body consists of individual members, and God has a wonderful plan for both the body and its members. Because it is God's will for the members to be in this body, then his will for the members should harmonize with his will for the body.[17]

This ideal scenario was broken in Corinth. To address the disunity, Paul borrows the body analogy from contemporary philosophers. Subsequent to this, body theology has become a popular description of the Christian church celebrating "diversity in unity and unity in diversity."[18]

Considering one another as different but important participants can be a useful analogy in dealing with disunity in a congregation. Paul tacks this teaching onto his discussion of how to express spiritual gifts. It's part of a broader section devoted to how we celebrate the Lord's supper and how to dress in church. His comments encourage individuals to see themselves as being part of a body.

Paul uses the word *soma* for body, lending vibrancy to his analogy and making it easier to envisage. It also conveys that the church is alive and in a constant state of change. The church is not an inanimate object.

He could have chosen another word, such as *organismos* ("organization") or *kormi* ("corpus, a collection"), but these would been inferior to *soma*. Although they convey the same general idea, they miss the implication of being alive.

The church is Christ's hands and feet on the earth. It represents Him. It's a manifestation of His resurrection, of His vitality.

---

[17] Fernando, *Reclaiming Friendship*, 150.
[18] Witherington, *Conflict and Community*, 254.

The church is a living, moving, developing structure inasmuch as it works together for the glory or honour of Christ. If the Corinthians pursued individual visions for the church, the church would suffer; it would no longer present Christ.

Paul suggests that the people try and see each other less as lone islands and more as a continent to be held together by Christ. The Corinthians, it would appear, were just as guilty of pursuing a self-centred postmodern agenda as we are today.

Ajith Fernando links how we embody Christ in our personal lives, speaking to our understanding of body theology. He points out that this was at the core of Christ's mission. The word becoming flesh was the greatest example of body theology in practice, as Jesus offered Himself sacrificially into the body of the church.[19]

This was Jesus's mission. It is also our mission, for like the Corinthians we are called to follow His example daily (Luke 9:23). Paul held to this, embodying himself with the characteristics of the groups he was trying to reach for Christ (1 Corinthians 9:20–22).

There is a close relationship then between the desires of the parts to be in harmony and the efforts of the parts to work together.

This key passage gives us a practical use of the body analogy:

If one part suffers, every part suffers with it; if one part is honored, every part rejoices with it. Now you are the body of Christ, and each one of you is a part of it. (1 Corinthians 12:26–27)

---

[19] Ajith Fernando, *Jesus Driven Ministry* (Wheaton, IL: Crossway, 2002), 17–29.

Rereading this gives me pause about my own friends in church. They challenge me to re-evaluate how I perceive my role in the body and how I see others. If the *soma* is alive, my relationships will be alive. This will be healthy for the church and its parts.

If we can begin to see each other as part of the same body that suffers together, breathes together, and experiences joy together, we might be inclined to pursue life with animation and feel less content with soulless relationships.

APPLICATION: BODY

- Take a look around at the congregation next time you're in church. Pray for those around you so you can see them as Christ does. See whether you can experience something of Paul's notion of a body of believers.
- Our challenge is for our hearts to grow in appreciation of those around us. We will have to let our theology for the body overwhelm the sensitivities of our feelings. Pray that God would give you the encouragement to want to grow.
- Pray that your church would have a clear vision of Christ at its heart. This is key for the body to harmonize and will be developed further as we look at 1 Corinthians 13.

In some of the spheres of ministry that I am involved in, we have people whose weaknesses bring much pain to my life. They misunderstand what we do and express their anger about our actions to others...

We stick to such people and willingly take on the frustration of talking with them because we believe that we will not ultimately lose through such costly commitment. It will be necessary for our theology to override our feelings on this. We must believe that we will be blessed if we pursue the implications of the biblical understanding of the body of Christ. To do this, of course, we must develop an approach to life where our theology is more important than our natural inclinations and instincts- a difficult task in this postmodern era![20]

—Ajith Fernando

---

[20] Ibid., 26–27.

Love

And yet I will show you the most excellent way.

¹ If I speak in the tongues of men or of angels, but do not have love, I am only a resounding gong or a clanging cymbal. ² If I have the gift of prophecy and can fathom all mysteries and all knowledge, and if I have a faith that can move mountains, but do not have love, I am nothing. ³ If I give all I possess to the poor and give over my body to hardship that I may boast, but do not have love, I gain nothing.

⁴ Love is patient, love is kind. It does not envy, it does not boast, it is not proud. ⁵ It does not dishonor others, it is not self-seeking, it is not easily angered, it keeps no record of wrongs. ⁶ Love does not delight in evil but rejoices with the truth. ⁷ It always protects, always trusts, always hopes, always perseveres.

⁸ Love never fails. But where there are prophecies, they will cease; where there are tongues, they will be stilled; where there is knowledge, it will pass away. ⁹ For we know in part and we prophesy in part, ¹⁰ but when completeness comes, what is in part disappears. ¹¹ When I was a child, I talked like a child, I thought like

a child, I reasoned like a child. When I became a man, I put the ways of childhood behind me. [12] For now we see only a reflection as in a mirror; then we shall see face to face. Now I know in part; then I shall know fully, even as I am fully known.

[13] And now these three remain: faith, hope and love. But the greatest of these is love.

Paul's epic chapter on sacrificial *agape* love is commonly read aloud at weddings, child dedications, and other important celebrations. It was originally written to a group but intended for individuals. It was written to distract the Corinthians from their disputes and inspire unity.

These verses have been described as showman-like. He was writing this way to divert his readers from the heat of the controversial topics in previous chapters. In oratory terms, such turns in style allow parties to cool off.

But we don't celebrate Paul's wise rhetoric in this passage. We celebrate its elegance and timelessness. As we read and reread his words, we must credit the author.

However we read this, we should view the passage as if we were among those disruptive Corinthian churchgoers. If we see Paul's words in their context, we will understand why he wrote of sacrificial love as the sinews and ligaments that hold the church body together despite differences of opinion.

The listening Corinthians would know that Paul's talk of tongues, prophecy, and knowledge addressed them directly. His talk of patience addressed those who were quick to anger. His talk of being kind addressed those caught up in esoterica who were forgetting the needful. At each point, he drew out the blood of Corinthian pride and replaced it with something more wholesome.

At the end, he highlights the contrast between the immature and the mature, the counterfeit and the genuine, the temporary and the eternal. When we meet Christ in eternity, faith and hope are no longer needed. But love—His love—remains.

Paul deconstructs the self-aggrandizement of the Corinthians and gives them an alternative mission: to embrace the notion of agape love. So rather than read the words from a corporate perspective, let's read them personally.

It's striking that *agape* love isn't defined by affection. It's defined by its resulting action. Read again 1 Corinthians 13:4–7 and appreciate that in each phrase *agape* love does something; it's not just a feeling. On an individual level, action is required for one to achieve unity and overcome disputes. Empathy alone won't work.

In an attempt to apply these verses to our lives, it's challenging to place one's own name into the definition of sacrificial love. It's too condemning, for we know that we fail to meet so many of these standards.

Rather than substitute our own names, another exercise is to try and substitute other character traits in place of love. A few words that work are generosity, courage, or grace. No substitute is perfect, but they help us to see the oft-repeated phrases in a new light.

In 1 Corinthians 13:9–12, Paul asserts that *agape* love comes with maturity. It comes with a fuller understanding. It is empowered by a more complete vision.

Maturity would be a good substitute for love in 1 Corinthians 13:4–7. Maturity in faith had come to Paul and he so wanted to encourage the Corinthians to embrace it as well.

Henri Nouwen, in a short book called *Life of the Beloved*, states that our spiritual awakening first occurs when we perceive that we are loved by God with *agape*. Although we are beloved by God, we do need to grow into His love, just as an adopted child grows into their acceptance by their family.[21] (pages 43–50).

Nouwen comes to a painful conclusion as he realizes that we don't often grow into our beloved status, in part because of our reluctance to grasp the obvious: our time here is limited. Instead of living for others and developing a legacy to be remembered, we work toward more self-centred goals.[22]

He encourages us to realize our maturity and give sacrificially, with *agape* love, for life is short and we will soon be with our Father.

Am I afraid to die? I am every time I let myself be seduced by the noisy voices of my world telling me that my "little life" is all I have and advising me to cling to it with all my might. But when I let these voices move to the background of my life and listen to that small soft voice calling me the Beloved, I know that there is

[21] Henri Nouwen, *Life of the Beloved* (New York, NY: Crossroads, 2002), 43–50.
[22] Ibid., 120–139.

nothing left to fear and that dying is the greatest act of love, the act that leads me into the eternal embrace of my God whose love is everlasting.[23]

Perhaps we live at our best when we know that our time here is brief and we exercise *agape* love like our Lord with courage, generosity, grace, and maturity—simply because He is calling us home. We live in the present for the future that awaits us.

APPLICATION: LOVE

- The first and second attributes of *agape* are patience and kindness. Pray that they would come to mind when your tolerance is tested.
- Paul takes the heat out of arguments by focusing on an inspiring spiritual truth, which is a useful lesson in itself. Pray that your church leaders would have the wisdom to seek such approaches when debates escalate.
- Nouwen's book and Paul's description of love call us to Christian maturity. Take a moment to think about what being more mature in your faith would look like for you and consider whether this is an earnest desire of your heart.

---

[23] Ibid., 139.

Prophecy

Follow the way of love and eagerly desire gifts of the Spirit, especially prophecy. [2] For anyone who speaks in a tongue does not speak to people but to God. Indeed, no one understands them; they utter mysteries by the Spirit. [3] But the one who prophesies speaks to people for their strengthening, encouraging and comfort. [4] Anyone who speaks in a tongue edifies themselves, but the one who prophesies edifies the church. [5] I would like every one of you to speak in tongues, but I would rather have you prophesy. The one who prophesies is greater than the one who speaks in tongues, unless someone interprets, so that the church may be edified.

[6] Now, brothers and sisters, if I come to you and speak in tongues, what good will I be to you, unless I bring you some revelation or knowledge or prophecy or word of instruction? [7] Even in the case of lifeless things that make sounds, such as the pipe or harp, how will anyone know what tune is being played unless there is a distinction in the notes? [8] Again, if the trumpet does not sound a clear call, who will get ready for battle? [9] So it is with you. Unless you speak intelligible

words with your tongue, how will anyone know what you are saying? You will just be speaking into the air. [10] Undoubtedly there are all sorts of languages in the world, yet none of them is without meaning. [11] If then I do not grasp the meaning of what someone is saying, I am a foreigner to the speaker, and the speaker is a foreigner to me. [12] So it is with you. Since you are eager for gifts of the Spirit, try to excel in those that build up the church.

[13] For this reason the one who speaks in a tongue should pray that they may interpret what they say. [14] For if I pray in a tongue, my spirit prays, but my mind is unfruitful. [15] So what shall I do? I will pray with my spirit, but I will also pray with my understanding; I will sing with my spirit, but I will also sing with my understanding. [16] Otherwise when you are praising God in the Spirit, how can someone else, who is now put in the position of an inquirer, say "Amen" to your thanksgiving, since they do not know what you are saying? [17] You are giving thanks well enough, but no one else is edified.

[18] I thank God that I speak in tongues more than all of you. [19] But in the church I would rather speak five intelligible words to instruct others than ten thousand words in a tongue.

[20] Brothers and sisters, stop thinking like children. In regard to evil be infants, but in your thinking be adults. [21] In the Law it is written: "With other

tongues and through the lips of foreigners I will speak to this people, but even then they will not listen to me, says the Lord."

²² Tongues, then, are a sign, not for believers but for unbelievers; prophecy, however, is not for unbelievers but for believers. ²³ So if the whole church comes together and everyone speaks in tongues, and inquirers or unbelievers come in, will they not say that you are out of your mind? ²⁴ But if an unbeliever or an inquirer comes in while everyone is prophesying, they are convicted of sin and are brought under judgment by all, ²⁵ as the secrets of their hearts are laid bare. So they will fall down and worship God, exclaiming, "God is really among you!"

When we give gifts, they are a sign of our affection, an indication of the strength of our gratitude or love toward the recipient. God bestows the gifts of the Spirit for similar reasons. We can be sure that He expects us to stand in respectful awe of His holy presents.

When we receive a gift, our reaction signifies our gratitude to the giver. What we do with the gift can speak to our personality. A precious gem might be hidden away by an introvert or put on display by an extrovert. Both value the gift while responding differently.

In this passage, Paul returns to the gifts of the Holy Spirit, discussing prophecy and speaking in tongues. He is concerned that the Corinthians don't demonstrate the type of behaviour he would expect from receiving such heavenly gifts. It seems many were displaying their giftings too frequently. At the very least, a few were being too effusive.

Paul also seems concerned about the perceived value of speaking in tongues. He doesn't rule out its use in corporate worship, but he writes that its edifying value is best realized in private. In contrast, he mentions the importance of prophecy as a means of both corporate and personal edification.

The word prophecy in the Greek is *propheteuo*, from *pro* ("before") and *phemi* ("tell"). The Old Testament prophets were those specially anointed by God to convey His will and foretell events. With the gift of the Holy Spirit, each Christian becomes a prophet.

> I have much more to say to you, more than you can now bear. But when he, the Spirit of truth, comes, he will guide you into all the truth. He will not speak on his own; he will speak only what he hears, and he will tell you what is yet to come. He will glorify me because it is from me that he will receive what he will make known to you. (John 16:12–14)

Although prophecy can mean more than teaching God's message, this is primarily what Paul writes about. He desires for the Corinthians to allow the Holy Spirit's gift to reveal God's mystery and penetrate their hearts so they will prophesy and teach it with clarity and sincerity. In this sense, prophecy is reserved for believers. It would be inappropriate for a non-Christian to teach or prophesy about Christ (1 Corinthians 14:22).

Prophecy can be a powerful evangelical tool. If a non-believer sees a Spirit-led Christian prophesy and their talk matches their walk, the prophecy becomes a powerful witness (1 Corinthians 14:24).

As for speaking in tongues, Paul is grateful to Christ for providing this amazing gift by which believers could speak with God in the language of their own hearts. He envisions it being used delicately and with discretion, since others won't necessarily benefit when we speak to God from our own hearts.

In contrast, our authenticity is powerful when we teach others and tell of His great love, especially when we consistently demonstrate this. Delivering His message can be as convicting as listening to the prophets of old.

APPLICATION: PROPHECY

- In the Old Testament, prophecy was shrouded in mystery and only available to those with a special anointing. Paul teaches that it's no longer a selective gift. Some are more gifted communicators and educators than others, yet we all have a valuable testimony. Consider your testimony and how you might explain it to an unbeliever without jargon.

- Listening for the Holy Spirit's teaching isn't easy, since we are readily distracted. In your devotions, take a moment to still your heart before you dive in. It should be as if you have noise-cancelling headphones on so you can better hear what's coming through (2 Timothy 2:21).

- Speaking in tongues might be a strange concept to some. For others, it may not be an accepted practice in their denomination. Paul affirms it for private use and explains how it can be used in corporate worship. Pray for a better understanding concerning tongues and the discretion to know when and if the gift should be used.

How can we have a heart that is receptive to the Spirit's prompting? Paul says we should examine ourselves before going to the Lord's supper (1 Cor 11:28). If so, how much more should we examine ourselves before leading God's people in worship or witness. Again Paul says, "Examine yourselves, to see whether you are in the faith. Test yourselves" (2 Cor. 13:5). The psalmist prayed, "Search me, O God, and know my heart! Try me and know my thoughts! And see if there be any grievous way in me, and lead me in the way everlasting!" (Ps 139:23–24)[24]

—Ajith Fernando

---

[24] Fernando, *Jesus Driven Ministry*, 35.

Edify

What then shall we say, brothers and sisters? When you come together, each of you has a hymn, or a word of instruction, a revelation, a tongue or an interpretation. Everything must be done so that the church may be built up. [27] If anyone speaks in a tongue, two—or at the most three—should speak, one at a time, and someone must interpret. [28] If there is no interpreter, the speaker should keep quiet in the church and speak to himself and to God.

[29] Two or three prophets should speak, and the others should weigh carefully what is said. [30] And if a revelation comes to someone who is sitting down, the first speaker should stop. [31] For you can all prophesy in turn so that everyone may be instructed and encouraged. [32] The spirits of prophets are subject to the control of prophets. [33] For God is not a God of disorder but of peace—as in all the congregations of the Lord's people.

[34] Women should remain silent in the churches. They are not allowed to speak, but must be in submission, as the law says. [35] If they want to inquire about

something, they should ask their own husbands at home; for it is disgraceful for a woman to speak in the church.

³⁶ Or did the word of God originate with you? Or are you the only people it has reached? ³⁷ If anyone thinks they are a prophet or otherwise gifted by the Spirit, let them acknowledge that what I am writing to you is the Lord's command. ³⁸ But if anyone ignores this, they will themselves be ignored.

³⁹ Therefore, my brothers and sisters, be eager to prophesy, and do not forbid speaking in tongues. ⁴⁰ But everything should be done in a fitting and orderly way.

I sometimes wonder which stories of Jesus's life Peter shared with Paul. Paul came to faith after Jesus's death and missed out on the discovery and wonder the other apostles enjoyed. Those stories would in time be written down, and today we have the benefit of walking with the disciples as the mysteries of God's will were revealed by Jesus.

In this passage, 1 Corinthians 14:26 reminds me of Peter's babbling about building a tent at the time of the transfiguration (Matthew 17). Peter, James, and John had just shared in this amazing scene, witnessing Moses and Elijah walk with Jesus, their friend and rabbi. The disciples heard God reaffirm His Son. It was a momentous occasion.

Ever the practical person, Peter wanted to encapsulate the experience. He wanted to build a proverbial snow globe to capture the memory so it might live on. He suggested they build tents so these great prophets would linger. This was his practical way of expressing amazement and wonder.

I would have loved to hear him tell Paul the full story.

We read in 1 Corinthians 14:26 that the church should have a similar response to Peter, one that seeks to build up and edify. The phrase "be built up" is translated from the Greek word *oikodome*, a composite word from *oikos*, which refers to a dwelling or house, and *doma*, which refers to the act of building.

Paul, like Peter, was practical and believed that expressions of Christian worship should seek to create, form, or build unity. This is an important prerequisite idea to understand; without it, some of the proceeding verses might seem contentious.

Paul summarizes this in 1 Corinthians 14:39, confirming that it wasn't his objective to stifle spirituality or restrict spiritual expression. However, he was keen to make sure that spirituality, when expressed, was done for the greater good of the church.

Some historical background might help us understand. The Greeks, and possibly many Corinthian converts, believed in pagan prophets, as well as priests who ministered to those prophets. It has been argued that Paul was keen to establish a different type of worship service than that offered by the contemporary polytheists. Rather than bringing questions to a prophetess, people were to reserve their questions for private discussion at home between husbands and wives (1 Corinthians 14:34–35).

According to Paul, a message from the Holy Spirit could be spoken by a prophet. But this prophetic word wasn't supposed to lead to an interview or interrogation of members of the congregation.

Paul thought that both men and women had been blessed to receive the gifts of the Spirit (1 Corinthians 12), so 1 Corinthians 14:34–35 doesn't represent a mandate to prevent women from participating in church services. Rather, we should understand these verses in context. People may have been indoctrinated by secular practice to expect women to question prophets. This was to be discouraged in Christian worship.

Although the Corinthians seemed to be making a hash of organized worship, they still had a strong foundation. They sought to make unabashed use of the gifts of the Holy Spirit and express them fervently and with passion.

As the size of the congregation had grown, however, this type of worship no longer built up unity in the church. Divisions were occurring between extroverts and introverts, and possibly between those who were quietly spiritual and those who were more about self-aggrandizement. To restore order and some semblance of spiritual reality—for all are equally sinners and equally saved before God in Christ—Paul provided them with guidelines for the expression of tongues and prophecy.

We don't go to church expecting to hear words of prophecy. Nor do we expect to hear tongues being spoken every Sunday morning. It's somewhat disappointing that we have, in the West, largely sterilized ourselves from the notions of spiritual communication; we expect only intellectual stimulation on Sunday mornings.

Even in these intellectual church services, we have an opportunity through singing, prayer, and private meditation to hear the calm, quiet voice of the Spirit. I suspect Paul would encourage us to listen and, when appropriate, share what we have heard.

For the edification of the church, however, that sharing might not take place in the middle of a service. It might happen later, in a small group, with one's spouse, or in the company of a good Christian friend.

The ministrations of the Spirit have never stopped being a gift. We should make sure we continue to share them.

APPLICATION: EDIFY

- Consider what you find edifying in the church. Is it the worship, the teaching, or the prayers? Perhaps it's all three. Pray that you would experience unity as the church celebrates each of these elements.
- It's worth remembering that we all have a role in edifying others. Pray that this would be in your heart, both while at church and in your regular life.
- Peter's suggestion to build tents at the transfiguration was not misplaced. It came from an inspired heart of worship. Pray for inspiration to better discern how you might perpetuate your moments with the Lord so they are longer-lasting.

Raised

Now, brothers and sisters, I want to remind you of the gospel I preached to you, which you received and on which you have taken your stand. [2] By this gospel you are saved, if you hold firmly to the word I preached to you. Otherwise, you have believed in vain.

[3] For what I received I passed on to you as of first importance: that Christ died for our sins according to the Scriptures, [4] that he was buried, that he was raised on the third day according to the Scriptures, [5] and that he appeared to Cephas, and then to the Twelve. [6] After that, he appeared to more than five hundred of the brothers and sisters at the same time, most of whom are still living, though some have fallen asleep. [7] Then he appeared to James, then to all the apostles, [8] and last of all he appeared to me also, as to one abnormally born.

[9] For I am the least of the apostles and do not even deserve to be called an apostle, because I persecuted the church of God. [10] But by the grace of God I am what I am, and his grace to me was not without effect. No, I worked harder than all of them—yet not I, but the grace of God that was with me. [11] Whether, then, it

is I or they, this is what we preach, and this is what you believed.

[12] But if it is preached that Christ has been raised from the dead, how can some of you say that there is no resurrection of the dead? [13] If there is no resurrection of the dead, then not even Christ has been raised. [14] And if Christ has not been raised, our preaching is useless and so is your faith. [15] More than that, we are then found to be false witnesses about God, for we have testified about God that he raised Christ from the dead. But he did not raise him if in fact the dead are not raised. [16] For if the dead are not raised, then Christ has not been raised either. [17] And if Christ has not been raised, your faith is futile; you are still in your sins. [18] Then those also who have fallen asleep in Christ are lost. [19] If only for this life we have hope in Christ, we are of all people most to be pitied.

[20] But Christ has indeed been raised from the dead, the firstfruits of those who have fallen asleep. [21] For since death came through a man, the resurrection of the dead comes also through a man. [22] For as in Adam all die, so in Christ all will be made alive. [23] But each in turn: Christ, the firstfruits; then, when he comes, those who belong to him. [24] Then the end will come, when he hands over the kingdom to God the Father after he has destroyed all dominion, authority and power. [25] For he must reign until he has put all his enemies under his feet. [26] The last enemy to be destroyed is death. [27] For he

"has put everything under his feet." Now when it says that "everything" has been put under him, it is clear that this does not include God himself, who put everything under Christ. [28] When he has done this, then the Son himself will be made subject to him who put everything under him, so that God may be all in all.

[29] Now if there is no resurrection, what will those do who are baptized for the dead? If the dead are not raised at all, why are people baptized for them? [30] And as for us, why do we endanger ourselves every hour? [31] I face death every day—yes, just as surely as I boast about you in Christ Jesus our Lord. [32] If I fought wild beasts in Ephesus with no more than human hopes, what have I gained? If the dead are not raised, "Let us eat and drink, for tomorrow we die."

[33] Do not be misled: "Bad company corrupts good character." [34] Come back to your senses as you ought, and stop sinning; for there are some who are ignorant of God—I say this to your shame.

Seeing someone walk and talk after being crucified and buried would cause quite a kerfuffle. To claim to have personally witnessed such events would be incredulous to most. But this was Paul's claim. He testified to having met a dead man, a man who was cold and motionless but had been reinvigorated with life.

This too was the testimony of the disciples who boldly spoke of how they met Jesus after He had died. They talked with Him, touched Him, and even ate breakfast with Him.

Jesus's resurrection isn't a readily believable aspect of our faith. If we think back though over the whole of His life, we'll find many equally incredible aspects. We can consider His conception, His visits from the Magi, His miracles, His healings. and His promises… and it's all miraculous.

In the context of an entire life filled with the inconceivable, the miracle of the resurrection is still a phenomenal event—but it fits with a phenomenal life. As such, perhaps it shouldn't stretch our faith any more than any other of the claims about Christ's life.

Paul's message to the Corinthians here isn't to reassert the validity of the resurrection. Given the people's Greco-Roman heritage, belief in the afterlife was entirely reasonable. In a way, their heritage made them more open to the idea than many are in the twenty-first century.

Instead of reasserting what was acceptable, Paul goes over some of the details of Christ's rising from the dead, details which had been altered by some of the Corinthians to be more palatable in terms of their cultural expectations.

Both the Greeks and Romans held to a belief in an afterlife for a person's spirit or soul. Some elements of Greek thought went further and proposed that the physical body was composed of evil matter. As such, it couldn't be taken to eternity. But the soul, being of the gods, was inherently divine and worthy to be saved.

For Christians to claim Christ had reappeared in human form after death was anathema to this line of thinking. A resurrected god wouldn't soil the divine nature of the human soul by clothing it again in human flesh.

To counter this philosophy, Paul emphasizes the bodily nature of Christ's resurrection (1 Corinthians 15: 3–8).

Some elements in the Corinthian church also diminished the miraculous nature of Christ's return to life, proposing that a person's new spiritual life, born into at conversion, was synonymous with resurrection. Thus, a believer's spiritual rebirth became their resurrection. In rising up from the waters of baptism, a believer was not only born again spiritually but resurrected to new life.

Into this falsehood, Paul writes of Christ rising from the dead. He didn't simply rise from the water but was crucified, killed, and buried. He resurrected from having been physically dead. This wasn't solely a spiritual rebirth, important though that aspect was; it was a physical reawakening from the dead, even though that was difficult to comprehend. (1 Corinthians 15:12–16).

Paul uses the Greek word *egeiro* to describe Christ's reawakening from death (1 Corinthians 15:12). Literally translated as "raised," it can also refer to being raised from sleep or illness, or simply having stood up after sitting or lying down. Paul uses *egeiro* to convey the active part of Jesus's resurrection. It implies an action, indicating that Christ's body actually moved.

When Paul refers to the resurrection (1 Corinthians 15:13), he uses a different word, the noun *anastases*, which can be translated as "standing again." This reinforces the notion that Jesus bodily rose. The resurrection wasn't solely a passing of the spirit into eternity; it was a re-emergence from the tomb in human form.

We shouldn't take lightly the lengths Paul goes to redress the Corinthians' tinkering with the resurrection story. Some in the congregation had adjusted his message to better suit their own beliefs, which is evidence enough that the resurrection was as hard a sell two thousand years ago as it remains today.

Opposition nowadays might also include denial of the afterlife. People may also question the reality of a physical resurrection and attempt to diminish the stark truth that we expect to be raised from the dead, not just from the waters of baptism.

Our defence of truth is different than it would have been for Paul. Our postmodern thinking demands the presentation of evidence and science to believe this miracle of miracles.

By definition, however, faith is being certain of something we don't see (Hebrews 11:1). In our faith, we therefore have to wait until heaven to fully comprehend Christ's resurrection glory. In between, we are afforded glimpses of His presence and are reassured by circumstantial evidence that confirms the resurrection of Christ to be a real event.[25]

Although facts may provide some intellectual reassurance, they do need to be processed and believed in order to enrich our faith.

We can acknowledge that we're married, since we have a certificate and remember the wedding day. We might also feel reassured by our partner's restatement of "I love you." What could be more convincing of the truth of our relationship? The richness of shared devotion over many years.

The same is true of one's belief in the resurrection. Both Paul's restatement of an early creed (1 Corinthians 15:3–8) and

---

[25] For further reading, see: Lee Strobel, *The Case for Christ* (Grand Rapids, MI: Zondervan, 1998), 191–258; and Frank Morison, *Who Moved the Stone?* (Grand Rapids, MI: Zondervan, 1987).

our many years of Easter celebrations are simple factual reminders. Our hearts, though, respond more to the years we have known Christ and been convinced that He is alive through His faithful care.

APPLICATION: RAISED

- Thank God for Easter Sunday. Perhaps focus on one detail and let this prompt your prayer.
- Think during the moments when you rise today. Whether you're raising yourself from lying down or being seated, think on Christ's rising. He *egireo* from death, not just from His resting place and not just from His tomb, but from death. Thank Him for this miracle.
- We talk of raising a glass to toast someone or in celebration of a special occasion. Raise a glass to Christ today for His reawakening from the grave.

Imperishable

But someone will ask, "How are the dead raised? With what kind of body will they come?" [36] How foolish! What you sow does not come to life unless it dies. [37] When you sow, you do not plant the body that will be, but just a seed, perhaps of wheat or of something else. [38] But God gives it a body as he has determined, and to each kind of seed he gives its own body. [39] Not all flesh is the same: People have one kind of flesh, animals have another, birds another and fish another. [40] There are also heavenly bodies and there are earthly bodies; but the splendor of the heavenly bodies is one kind, and the splendor of the earthly bodies is another. [41] The sun has one kind of splendor, the moon another and the stars another; and star differs from star in splendor.

[42] So will it be with the resurrection of the dead. The body that is sown is perishable, it is raised imperishable; [43] it is sown in dishonor, it is raised in glory; it is sown in weakness, it is raised in power; [44] it is sown a natural body, it is raised a spiritual body.

If there is a natural body, there is also a spiritual body. [45] So it is written: "The first man Adam became a living being"; the last Adam, a life-giving spirit. [46] The spiritual did not come first, but the natural, and after that the spiritual. [47] The first man was of the dust of the earth; the second man is of heaven. [48] As was the earthly man, so are those who are of the earth; and as is the heavenly man, so also are those who are of heaven. [49] And just as we have borne the image of the earthly man, so shall we bear the image of the heavenly man.

[50] I declare to you, brothers and sisters, that flesh and blood cannot inherit the kingdom of God, nor does the perishable inherit the imperishable. [51] Listen, I tell you a mystery: We will not all sleep, but we will all be changed—[52] in a flash, in the twinkling of an eye, at the last trumpet. For the trumpet will sound, the dead will be raised imperishable, and we will be changed. [53] For the perishable must clothe itself with the imperishable, and the mortal with immortality. [54] When the perishable has been clothed with the imperishable, and the mortal with immortality, then the saying that is written will come true: "Death has been swallowed up in victory."

[55] "Where, O death, is your victory? Where, O death, is your sting?"

[56] The sting of death is sin, and the power of sin is the law. [57] But thanks be to God! He gives us the victory through our Lord Jesus Christ.

[58] Therefore, my dear brothers and sisters, stand firm. Let nothing move you. Always give yourselves

fully to the work of the Lord, because you know that
your labor in the Lord is not in vain.

In Oxfordshire, England, a recent archaeological find surprised
historians. A whole egg was unearthed from a wet bog that dat-
ed back to the Roman era, two thousand years ago. The person
excavating the site found a clutch of eggs with perfectly preserved
shells in an old Roman well in Aylesbury. In removing the eggs
from their resting place, at least one cracked. The odour confirmed
that the inside hadn't been so well preserved as the outside.

The next challenge for the archaeological team was to determine how to extract the contents to find out what kind of bird had
laid the eggs—and to do so without damaging the shell of the only
egg that had remained intact.

This represents the reverse scenario of what some in the
Corinthian church believed would happen to the dead. For them,
it was easy to believe in the preservation of the internal soul. This
wasn't a difficult leap based on their pre-Christian beliefs. The
challenge was in believing that the body, the outer shell, might
survive intact in eternity.

Paul's focus in the initial verses of 1 Corinthians 15 is the resurrection of Christ. He then switched to the resurrection of the
Corinthians themselves.

Paul says that it's foolish to deliberate too much over the finer points of salvation. Nevertheless, he placates the Corinthians'
anxieties with helpful analogies.

There is wisdom in this approach, for it can be destructive
to ruminate greatly over matters we cannot fathom. Most people

don't plan beyond the foreseeable future, let alone into eternity. Some, if they're foresighted, make financial provision. Others might invest time and effort in their education. But many of us are hard-stretched to plan beyond the next week or month.

Like the Corinthians, we spend too much time worrying over the transient matters of day-to-day life and don't worry enough about planning our later years. Rather than accept that God, in His divinity, has resolved the aging problem of our bodies, we fret. In our unbelief, we miss out on the expectation of a marvellous new life on an amazing new earth.

Conversely, if we grasp this concept of a new life on a new earth, it could very well distract us from living our lives. We might be too otherworldly to be of any worldly use.

Paul tackled this precise problem with those who had fallen into such a trap in the Thessalonian church. Some there had become so fervent in their anticipation of Christ's return that they'd become like startled rabbits in a car's headlights (2 Thessalonians 3:6–13), paralyzed and no longer functioning in the ways Paul expected of Christians.

In grasping hold of a future imperishable life, we should not be distracted.

For imperishable, Paul uses the word *aphthartos*, the antonym to *phtheiro* ("to shrivel or whither, to ruin or corrupt"). *Aphthartos* is all about being impervious to decay.

As sophisticated twenty-first-century Christians, we must not fear believing in an eternal life, realized on a new earth and with an imperishable body. As surely as Christ rose from the dead on the first Easter Sunday, these promises will be upheld.

But ours is a cynical world, desperately short on any acknowledgement of the divine. Our challenge is to find ways to live our eternal perspective so it becomes our daily reality. This puts us in the world but not of it. We aren't paralyzed by our anticipation of eternal life but given purpose by it.

At my own conversion, the parable of the prodigal son was of great personal reassurance. Knowing that I was accepted by the Father unconditionally and without expectation removed a great deal of anxiety about what it meant to be a Christian. I revisit that parable often, especially when I'm concerned about something that is beyond comprehension in the Bible.

Returning now to that story, I am reminded that eternity awaits the return of God's sons and daughters. The finer details of our lives there are yet to be discovered. In the meantime, we should rejoice and continue to walk homeward with purpose and vision, and with less anxiety.

APPLICATION: IMPERISHABLE

- Eschatology, or the study of the end-times, forms a small part of our belief system as Christians. Grace, forgiveness, and hope are much more dominant elements. Dedicate a few moments of prayer to thank God for His complete redemptive plan.
- Spiritual matters, like our resurrection, are challenging. It's one thing to confess to the resurrection of our Lord, but quite another to conceive of our own. Take time to pray to the Holy Spirit that He might bring

insight, encouragement, and belief that these things will come to pass.

- We often use the word perishable to describe fresh produce, whereas nonperishable describes preserved goods. Next time you shop for groceries, select a nonperishable item and thank Jesus that through His grace you too are now imperishable.

Time

Now about the collection for the Lord's people: Do what I told the Galatian churches to do. [2] On the first day of every week, each one of you should set aside a sum of money in keeping with your income, saving it up, so that when I come no collections will have to be made. [3] Then, when I arrive, I will give letters of introduction to the men you approve and send them with your gift to Jerusalem. [4] If it seems advisable for me to go also, they will accompany me.

[5] After I go through Macedonia, I will come to you—for I will be going through Macedonia. 6 Perhaps I will stay with you for a while, or even spend the winter, so that you can help me on my journey, wherever I go. [7] For I do not want to see you now and make only a passing visit; I hope to spend some time with you, if the Lord permits. [8] But I will stay on at Ephesus until Pentecost, [9] because a great door for effective work has opened to me, and there are many who oppose me.

[10] When Timothy comes, see to it that he has nothing to fear while he is with you, for he is carrying on the work of the Lord, just as I am. [11] No one, then, should

treat him with contempt. Send him on his way in peace so that he may return to me. I am expecting him along with the brothers.

¹² Now about our brother Apollos: I strongly urged him to go to you with the brothers. He was quite unwilling to go now, but he will go when he has the opportunity.

¹³ Be on your guard; stand firm in the faith; be courageous; be strong. ¹⁴ Do everything in love.

¹⁵ You know that the household of Stephanas were the first converts in Achaia, and they have devoted themselves to the service of the Lord's people. I urge you, brothers and sisters, ¹⁶ to submit to such people and to everyone who joins in the work and labors at it.

Two words in Greek were used to express time: *kairos* and *chronos*. *Kairos* identifies a moment, like in Ecclesiastes 3, which refers to seasons epitomized by a prevailing mood. *Chronos* is used to refer instead to a quantifiable period of time.

In 1 Corinthians 16:7, Paul uses *chronos*. He wishes to spend a considerable period with the Corinthians. His visit won't coincide with a particular moment, but he intends to invest more hours, days, weeks, or months into his ministry with them.

Other issues are mentioned in this passage, including the gathering of an offering, a possible return of Apollos, and the pending arrival of Timothy. These points speak to Paul's commitment to the Corinthians, who remain dear to his heart despite the matters arising in the preceding fifteen chapters.

Ministry takes time—to teach, listen, hear, and grow. At the time of Paul's writing, approximately three years had passed since he had left Corinth. The church had developed in the intervening years. As these early Christians applied their new faith, they'd taken some wrong turns. Paul knew them well enough to set them back on the right path, but it would take more than one letter. It would take a personal visit to redirect, re-engage, and reassure them of their salvation.

Time was precious to Paul, for he was impassioned by mission and wished to take the gospel to places where Christ hadn't been previously preached, perhaps to Spain or even beyond. In that context, it must have taxed Paul to return to old ground. However, he was wise enough to understand the necessity of such journeys, since Corinth wasn't the only church to receive a repeat visit. Paul's second and third missionary journeys convey how seriously he regarded mission follow-up.

Time is precious for us too, even more so as we age. Paul's readiness to volunteer more time to the errant fold of Corinth is a challenge for us to do likewise when circumstances test our patience. As with Paul, ministry for the Christian should be perpetual. Provided we are living in the Lord, it never really stops. All we do is ministry.

We might say, "Ministry is time and time is ministry." But occasionally we forget this and neglect to go before God and make sure we spend our wisely and in accordance with His wishes.

Although returning to Corinth went against Paul's master plan to reach distant lands, he was ready to forgo those plans. He must have perceived God's will and received the Lord's blessing to put his larger mission aside.

There are lessons for us in this, whether it be to reflect on how we spend our time in ministry or how often we seek God's blessing on how we spend our days. Let us hope we can be as God-seeking and wise as Paul.

APPLICATION: TIME

- Consider your roles in ministering the gospel, whatever form that may take. Hold this time before God and ask for His direction.
- Our lives as Christians are a reflection of how important we perceive the gospel to be. Consider whether you could give more time to ministry or whether He could better use your time.
- Ministry is time and time is ministry. This is true if we are living for the Lord. Pray that this would be true today, and that it may become true every day.

Be Mature

Be on your guard; stand firm in the faith; be courageous; be strong. [14] Do everything in love.

[15] You know that the household of Stephanas were the first converts in Achaia, and they have devoted themselves to the service of the Lord's people. I urge you, brothers and sisters, [16] to submit to such people and to everyone who joins in the work and labors at it. [17] I was glad when Stephanas, Fortunatus and Achaicus arrived, because they have supplied what was lacking from you. [18] For they refreshed my spirit and yours also. Such men deserve recognition.

[19] The churches in the province of Asia send you greetings. Aquila and Priscilla greet you warmly in the Lord, and so does the church that meets at their house. [20] All the brothers and sisters here send you greetings. Greet one another with a holy kiss.

[21] I, Paul, write this greeting in my own hand.

[22] If anyone does not love the Lord, let that person be cursed! Come, Lord!

[23] The grace of the Lord Jesus be with you.

[24] My love to all of you in Christ Jesus. Amen.

How does one finish a letter like 1 Corinthians? Prior to Paul's characteristic farewells, he issues four commands. His instructions here have been likened to military orders and are proceeded by his request for the Corinthians to love one another with *agape* love.

Here are his four commands: be alert, stand firm, act courageously, and be strong. The military implication is clear, since each term would be familiar to any soldier. At the end of his correspondence, he once again acknowledges the conflict in Corinth; addressing it will require military discipline.

Paul urges the people to be alert—or more accurately, to rise to the challenges they face. He asks them to stand firm and hold resolutely to his teachings.

They are also to be courageous. In fact, the word he uses is *andrizo*, which is best rendered as "act like men" or "be mature." For the ancients, being mature was exemplified by courage. A manly soldier was one who fought courageously.

Finally, he orders the Corinthians to be strong, to feel empowered by the truth of the gospel. He hopes that their dedication to pursuing the purity of the gospel will strengthen their resolve to continue the ministry.

We read then of some examples of Corinthians who appear to have taken these instructions to heart. Paul holds up Stephanas, Fortunatus, and Achaicus, individuals who are worthy enough to be well-received by their congregation.

He also encourages his readers to join in the work of ministry (1 Corinthians 15:16). Their participation will help build relationships in the church. The work will not be easy, for they would need to labour. In other words, they will have to work like adults.

Finally, he writes that being as mature as Stephanas and his colleagues will require the people to submit to the authority of others. As he notes in 1 Corinthians 16:18, *"Such men deserve recognition."*

No doubt this last picture of maturity caused a stir among the Corinthians rebels. Though mature soldiers will follow the orders of their commanders without question, less mature soldiers are less willing to trust the instructions they're given.

Paul's desire is to foster a spirit of unity in the church of Christ, and in doing so bring honour and respectability to the church. Mark 3:25 reminds us, *"If a house is divided against itself, that house cannot stand."*

From these closing verses, let's take a moment to reflect on the hardships of ministry. Success requires incredible maturity, even more *andrizo* than for a soldier. It would be more accurate to write that the strength and resolve for ministry requires superhuman input. In other words, it must be supernaturally driven and Jesus-led.

We will close as Paul does: *"My love to all of you in Christ Jesus. Amen."* In this way, he reminds us of the centrality of Christ to his church.

APPLICATION: BE MATURE

- It's hard not to react defensively when we are verbally attacked or our ideas are discounted in ministry meetings. But maturity demands that we stay our natural reactions. Pray that Jesus would help you to take a pause when you perceive a personal injury.

- Ministry is hard work. Consider how you might encourage a ministry worker this week.
- Being mature doesn't only require us to listen and stay quiet. It will probably involve being submissive to the ideas and direction of others. Pray for the discernment to know when to stand firm and when to follow.

Reflections

> If I fought wild beasts in Ephesus with no more than human hopes, what have I gained? (1 Corinthians 15:32)

In this book's introduction, we discussed the idea that Paul's ministry in Corinth, the gateway to the Achaian peninsula, was like the wake a boat leaves in the sea. We imagined the good news of Christ sweeping over this bustling cosmopolitan city and leaving behind an opportunity for people to have a fresh start. We reflected on Paul's wish to see that the wake he left, the channel he carved, remained true to the gospel.

Let's return to this useful analogy. It conveys the notion of pure direction and a clear course.

Paul's impetus to write to the Corinthians was in some sense good news. It meant there were newcomers there who hadn't benefitted from his teaching during his first visit. He might also have needed to write to others who had short memories and had forgotten the fundamentals.

His text reinforced the wake of the boat amidst choppy waters. Quite a few swells had arisen in the water, encroaching upon the wake. Into these rough seas, Paul preached once again the centrality of the cross, the purity of the resurrection, and the need for *agape* love. His goal was to re-establish truth where its purity had become uncertain and unstable.

I have experienced the importance of staying within the wake of a large boat. My wife and I once took a holiday to the west coast of Scotland. The village of Tayvallich is perched on Loch Sween, a narrow strip of sea between two narrow extensions of the Kintyre peninsula.

We decided to take a daytrip down the loch to Castle Sween. In calm waters, this is a straightforward trip, sixteen kilometres each way. We took a small speedboat and jet ski and enjoyed the ride without any issues.

After a sunny picnic on the beach with some free-roaming highland cows, we set off for home. By late afternoon when we left the beech, however, a brisk wind had picked up. The larger speed boat was carrying most of the family and made good progress against the wind and waves.

I was on the jet ski and it struggled in the swell. The only way the jet ski made any headway was to hunker in behind the speedboat and use the flattened wake. If the jet ski erred too far to the right or left, or if it fell back, the waves forced it into the air. It would fall further and further behind.

This was a stern lesson in seamanship, as well as a useful picture of what was happening in Corinth. Too many individuals were trying to ride their metaphorical jet skis outside the wake of the church. Now they were in danger of being left behind—or worse, becoming lost at sea. Paul wrote so they could climb back aboard to collectively navigate through the storms with unity.

When we act as individuals, choosing to leave the wake of the church to travel choppy waters, we disregard the preciousness of the church. Its value becomes so meaningless to us that we are to dispense with it. And we do it at arguably the most important time, when the seas are rough.

Into this situation, Paul called the Corinthians to value the body of the church and the fellowship they experienced there. He called them back and brought them together.

This idea is teased out in 1 Corinthians 15:32, which speaks to the importance of retaining what we've learned from our faith when circumstances are difficult.

Paul had also experienced opposition in Ephesus, where it was so vociferous that he referred to it as being like a wild beast.

In 1 Corinthians 15:32, Paul wrote of metaphorical beasts that would ravage the gospel, tear it apart, and shred its outer garments all for the sake of suppressing the power of its message.

This is an interesting way to describe false teaching and naysayers.

Although subtle attacks on the purity of the gospel may seem innocuous, they can have the same ferocity, and same ends, as a wild beast's attack, especially if such attacks are allowed to proceed unchecked.

We should admire Paul's response to these metaphorical beasts. His first letter to the Corinthians can help us decipher his motives, enabling us to see his perspectives on polemic issues. We can be gracious to some of the language he uses, for it was never meant to be offensive or controversial.

Paul saw individuals leaving the wake of the boat in rough seas and reasoned that the use of human effort, human argumentation, and human persuasiveness would undermine his reliance on Christ, and therefore his standing as a sent apostle. So he determined not to rely on his humanity.

Instead he referred to Jesus. He chose to depend on God as opposed to his own human hopes—*"no more than human hopes"* (1 Corinthians 15:32), the Greek phrase for which is *ei kaka anthropon*.

Paul's point was that if we only deal with our conflicts with human methods, whether they come from the church or the wider community, what have we learned? How mature have we become?

Paul's wish, and by extension Christ's, is that we would rely on the message of the cross and on the tools of the gospel. This is the wake that we are to return to.

The letter of 1 Corinthians was written to address church conflicts, but it is also a book of hope—hope that those who had received the Holy Spirit would hear and respond to Paul's call. The letter has weight and substance that goes beyond the well-known passages about love and the gifts of the spirit. It was written to keep a congregation on track, in the wake of the gospel. It forces us to revisit so many fundamentals of our faith: the cross, the resurrection, eternity, the Holy Spirit, communion, and church behaviour.

On finishing this book, I feel pulled back into the wake of the boat which Paul was navigating for our heavenly Father. This boat is taking us home surely and safely, not using human means but relying on God's grace and guidance.

For Further Reading

William Barclay, *The New Daily Study Bible: The Letters to the Corinthians* (Louisville, KY: Westminster John Knox Press, 2002).

Ben Witherington III, *Conflict and Community in Corinth: A Sociorhetorical Commentary on 1 and 2 Corinthians* (Grand Rapids, MI: William B Eerdmans, 1995).

Craig Blomberg, 1 Corinthians: NIV Application Commentary (Grand Rapids, MI: Zondervan, 1994).

The Greek translations in this book have been paraphrased from material found at: "Verse by Verse Commentary by Book," *Precept Austin.* Date of access: August 16, 2023 (www.preceptaustin.org/verse_by_verse).

Further Reading

Proceeds from the sales of this book will be donated to St. Timothy's Christian Classical Academy, Ottawa and LOCAL Church, Ottawa.

ST. TIMOTHY'S CHRISTIAN CLASSICAL ACADEMY, OTTAWA

St. Timothy's is a small interdenominational Christian school with students from Senior Kindergarten to Grade Eight. It was founded by a group of Christian families in 2005. It is a charitable organization and seeks to offer classical education in a Christian environment to children from a broad range of backgrounds. This is achieved through generous provision of tuition assistance.

The dedicated faculty at St Timothy's seeks to lead their students to revere truth, desire goodness, and rejoice in beauty. The school has been housed in several locations throughout Ottawa since its inception but would ideally seek to establish a home for itself.

In the meantime, the school continues to be a beacon for Christ in the inner city. St. Timothy's strives to bless children, parents, and the broader community so as to fulfill the ambassadorial role that Paul strove for in his pupil Timothy.

Further details can be found online: www.st-timothys.ca

LOCAL CHURCH, OTTAWA

Dr. Small and his family attend LOCAL Church, Ottawa, which was established in 2018. It is twinned with its sister campus in Tauranga Moana in New Zealand.

The church preaches and professes a Christ-focused message. It has generous ministries in local and international charitable giving. LOCAL promotes the benefits of small group discipleship ministry.

More details of the ministry and work of the church can be found online: www.localchurch.co

A WORD FROM HIS WORD
BY GARY R. SMALL

Each chapter of *A Word from His Word* focuses on a single word or phrase from a short biblical passage. It is the author's prayer that by returning to a simplified but effective approach to Bible reading, your daily times with God's word will be invigorated. Enjoy the entire series!

NOW AVAILABLE:

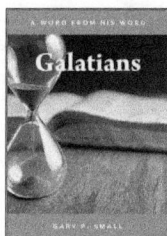

Galatians	*1&2 Thessalonians*
Ephesians	*1&2 Timothy*
Philipians	*Philemon & Titus*
Colossians	

COMING SOON:

Romans
2 Corinthians

www.ingramcontent.com/pod-product-compliance
Lightning Source LLC
La Vergne TN
LVHW051408080426
835508LV00022B/2987